The Joy of Connections

The Joy of Connections

100 Ways to Beat
Loneliness and Live
a Happier and More
Meaningful Life

Dr. Ruth K. Westheimer

with Allison Gilbert *and* Pierre Lehu

RODALE
NEW YORK

Published in the United States by Rodale Books,
an imprint of Random House, a division of
Penguin Random House LLC, New York.

Rodale & Plant with colophon is a registered trademark of
Penguin Random House LLC.

Hardback ISBN 978-0-593-73622-7
Ebook ISBN 978-0-593-73623-4

Printed in the United States of America on acid-free paper

rodalebooks.com | randomhousebooks.com

2 4 6 8 9 7 5 3 1

First Edition

Book design by Susan Turner

It is not good for a human being to be alone.

—Genesis 2:18

Contents

Introduction

———

L ONELINESS IS ABOUT THE QUALITY OF CONNECTIONS in your life, not the quantity.

Unlike solitude, which can be sought-after and peaceful, loneliness stems from a sense of social isolation. You might be surrounded by people from morning to night, but if you feel invisible to them, like you don't matter, you will likely feel alone. Similarly, if you believe that you have nobody to call in an emergency or to water your plants when you go on vacation, you might feel particularly adrift and disconnected.

The reason loneliness is painful is that human beings are social creatures by nature and our health depends on these relationships. When we're lonely, serious health conditions may arise. Loneliness is associated with an increased risk of stroke, confusion and memory loss, and cardiovascular disease. It may shorten our lives, as much as smoking up to fifteen cigarettes a day, and is even more harmful than being sedentary and significantly overweight.

But loneliness is subjective. It's a *feeling*. And because it's a feeling, there's plenty we can do to alleviate it.

You can make the decision that being lonely is no longer an option. You can pursue relationships that make you feel special and appreciated. I want you to know that it's possible to choose a fuller, richer path right now.

I know this is true from my work and my life. And it's why at age ninety-six I couldn't sit idly by when so many are suffering. If you've sunk into the swamp of loneliness, you may feel like it's impossible to get out. Take my hand. Let me pull you out of the muck.

When New York State governor Kathy Hochul appointed me Ambassador to Loneliness, the first such position in the United States, she couldn't have chosen someone with better credentials. I've been sleeping with loneliness my entire life.

I've known the loneliness of being separated from my family at the age of ten, becoming a refugee, and never seeing my parents or grandparents again. I've known the loneliness of illness and disability, the kind that crashes over you when your body has been pierced by shrapnel and you've been severely wounded in a bomb blast, have lost part of your foot, and are sure you're about to die. I've also known the loneliness of feeling unchangeably other. While my four-foot-seven height has always been a punch line on late-night television, and while being shorter than most everyone else has surely helped me stand out professionally, it's also been profoundly isolating. I often thought that no man would ever want me and that I'd never get married. But I did manage to get married, three times, in fact. The first two marriages ended in divorce and the third, to Fred Westheimer, lasted thirty-five years, until he passed away; he was the love of my life.

I'll let you in on a little secret: My personal experiences with loneliness aren't the only reasons I was named Ambassador to Loneliness. The appointment happened because I lobbied for it. I pushed for the role because I knew that my background as a sex therapist made me uniquely qualified to help people overcome loneliness. Sexual dysfunction and loneliness both carry stigma. Nobody is excited to admit they're having difficulty in the bedroom. Nobody is thrilled to confess they have too few reliable friends. Shame is the thread that connects them both, and shame is what I've always tried to help people overcome. Think back to the 1980s. The humiliation gay people felt during the AIDS crisis was wholly avoidable. It's why I always spoke so openly about homosexuality, embracing all expressions of love. I tried hard to change the conversation about sex and belonging during *that* epidemic, and I know that if we talk openly about loneliness—unapologetically and without euphemisms—those who are feeling painfully disconnected will feel less alone, too.

That loneliness is now an epidemic is widely known. Studies have been done and books have been written. Media coverage has exposed the vastness of the problem. I applaud all those who've undertaken this reporting and research. But, as I've mentioned, I offer a different and much-needed perspective. This is not a book about how society has arrived at such a tender and precarious place. This is not a book that examines the government's efforts to resolve the crisis (though at the end of this book U.S. Surgeon General Dr. Vivek Murthy offers important strategies for feeling more socially connected).

My training is as a behavioral therapist. When I saw clients in my office, I didn't spend time delving into their past, trying to figure out the root cause of their sexual problems. I left that to the psychologists and psychiatrists. My work was much more direct and fast-moving. I simply helped anyone who came to see me—or listened to me on the radio or watched me on TV—have better sex by modifying how they engaged in sex. And this is the approach that I am taking with *The Joy of Connections*. If you are lonely, what you need is practical advice on beating back this scourge, and this is what I am going to provide.

The Joy of Connections offers a straightforward road

map for overcoming loneliness—one hundred concrete ideas and opportunities that can be acted upon immediately. The guidance is based on tactics I've used myself and in my private practice, some with clients who were quite lonely. I also include lessons from organizational psychologist and Wharton professor Adam Grant; founding director of the MIT Initiative on Technology and Self, Sherry Turkle; bestselling author and *Happier* podcast host Gretchen Rubin; and others.

But I'm not only giving you advice. I'm going to do the best I can to push you into *taking my advice*.

I'm going to be a cheerleader, a coach, and a drill sergeant, all rolled into one. Everyone who knows me quickly finds out that when I want something, I want it now, maybe even yesterday. Of course, some things you have to wait for, but in my life, I've found that waiting patiently often means that you don't get what you want. And since having some chutzpah is what it takes to make it in this world, we must apply this same type of agency to the problem of loneliness. Because while loneliness is a terrible thing, as I can attest to, it's also a condition that can be beaten back. And while I would never say that it will be easy, I will absolutely state that it's possible.

Dr. Ruth's Menu
for Connection

S IMILAR TO THE COLORFUL PLATE THE USDA USES TO
recommend which food groups should be consumed for a healthy lifestyle, my Menu for Connection represents the parts of our life that require the
most care and attention for building and nurturing meaningful relationships. I created this simple framework to
translate decades of scholarly research on human connections and happiness into guidance that you can use
right now.

Instead of fruits, grains, vegetables, protein, and a
small serving of dairy, I've developed one hundred empowering ideas and strategies and divided eighty-eight of them
into five parts: "Self," "Family," "Friends and Lovers," "Community," and a small portion of "Technology." Each is an
essential element of the Menu for Connection. The final
twelve strategies are presented in "Your Monthly Calendar"

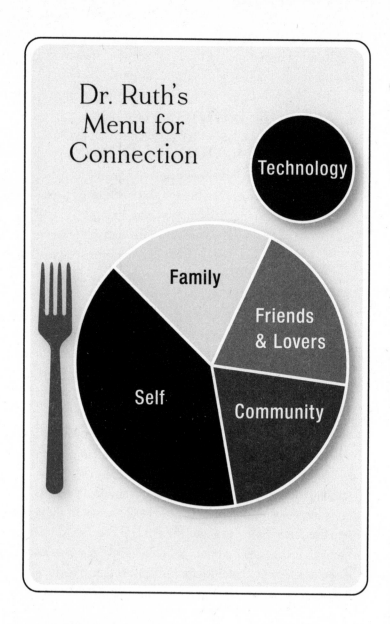

Dr. Ruth's
Menu for
Connection

Technology

Family

Friends
& Lovers

Self

Community

because there are times of the year that offer specific opportunities for building joy and relationships.

While I will explain each portion of the Menu for Connection at the opening of each section, it is important to note that the largest piece, the one that purposefully contains the most opportunities, is "Self." If you are struggling with loneliness and are ready to make positive changes in how you interact with others, you must first determine what it is about your outlook or behavior that has made you retreat into yourself or push people away. This is not easy to do, but your relationships are more likely to flourish once you put in the work.

Loneliness is an individual experience, and I recognize that each and every page may not resonate, as what's obvious to you might be illuminating and life-changing to someone else. Some concepts are for those who need help finding and making connections; others are for individuals who already have connections but want help deepening them. My hope is that you'll take away what you need and transform your relationships based on the cumulative nature of the Menu for Connection.

Let's get to work!

Self

WHILE IT MAY SEEM THAT EVERYONE AROUND you is fulfilled by their relationships, the truth is that most people experience loneliness at some point in their lives. Let that sink in. It's likely that most everyone you know, everyone in your neighborhood, everyone you walk by on the street, has felt the pangs of loneliness. A recent Meta-Gallup survey shows that nearly one in four adults around the world—more than one billion people—don't feel fully connected to others.

Ever since U.S. Surgeon General Dr. Vivek Murthy proclaimed loneliness an epidemic in the United States, there's been a flurry of activity to help people feel less alone. Legislation has been introduced in Congress to establish an Office of Social Connection Policy to advise the president. The World Health Organization launched the Commission on Social Connection. Mayors across the country have demanded funding to support more mental health programs in their cities and the staff to run them. And New York State governor Kathy Hochul appointed me Ambassador to Loneliness!

I lost my family in the Holocaust, and I could not have felt any lonelier because of that. While eventually I created a family in the typical sense, finding a life partner and having children and grandchildren, I never stopped pulling together a wider "chosen" family. I curated these bonds with absolute purpose. I went out of my way to find these friends and knit them together. And in doing so I became less lonely.

But getting to that point was hard. I grew up in an orphanage and was surrounded every minute of every day by other children. There was no privacy whatsoever! Yet on July 12, 1945, I confessed in my diary:

Above all, I'm longing for a friend.

And the next day, I wrote:

I live with 150 people—and am alone.

I now know what my seventeen-year-old self didn't yet understand. Loneliness has nothing to do with the number of people around you. If you're not meaningfully connected, if there's no substance to your interactions, you will likely feel insignificant and unseen. But you can bring loneliness to its knees. Unlike a fatal disease, loneliness, I've learned, is curable.

In my view, the key to ridding your life of loneliness resides inside you. As a therapist, I've sat across from many clients who faced very real hardships and disabilities, and I was able to help most of them. But I could never make the kinds of changes they needed *for* them; I could only *guide* them. Therapists are expert advisers. It's the individual seeking a new road who must take action.

But changing patterns of behavior takes effort. And this is why "Self" is the most important component of the Menu for Connection. You must pay attention to your thoughts, feelings, and actions, the ones that are holding you back from making the types of connections you most want. Self-awareness leads to coping strategies and solutions, builds self-esteem and confidence, and smooths communication with others so that you can nurture and maintain healthy relationships. With reflection, you're able to identify areas for improvement and follow through with your aspirations.

So let's begin by focusing our attention where it's likely the hardest and most uncomfortable, but also where success is solely within your power: on yourself.

Look in the Mirror

The first step to fixing any problem is to admit that it exists. If loneliness is what is affecting you, then what better way to face your problem than to stand in front of a mirror and say it out loud? You may feel silly, you may cry, but having the problem out in the open is your first step toward making the necessary changes to become less lonely. Reading this book is proof to me that you're aware of what's causing you pain and you're open to solutions. I have no doubt you're on your way to building the kinds of connections you most want!

I've faced many difficult challenges in my life, as you'll come to see as you read on. During a visit to Paris, where I had studied psychology at the Sorbonne in the early 1950s, I saw in a shop a ruby-red decorative sign for sale that immediately caught my eye. The words "It CAN be done" were emblazoned in English across the front in bright gold lettering. I didn't buy it, but the owner of the store later sent it to me as a gift. He had noticed how much I admired it. The sign has been my treasure ever since, for more than forty years. I look at it whenever I feel discouraged.

What's the difference between complaining to yourself that you're lonely and saying it out loud? I've been a therapist throughout my career and can tell you that my clients began to heal the moment they admitted to having a problem. The road ahead will be hard, but just keep going. You are getting closer to feeling less alone and isolated. *It CAN be done.*

Make Peace with Yourself

You will not be able to sustain healthy relationships if you don't love yourself first. No friend or sexual partner can do all that emotional heavy lifting for you, and worse, you might build walls around yourself that are so high that you'll prevent anyone from scaling them.

I am not suggesting you brainwash yourself into thinking that you're a gorgeous model if you're not, and I am not asking you to ignore physical or mental disabilities that make your life more difficult. Brushing off hardship is not what I'm saying to do. My advice is to gradually accept what makes you different and begin relationship-building from there. To do this—and I realize that I am biased as a lifelong therapist—you might consider professional counseling.

As I write these words, I do, in fact, love myself, but I had a very hard time being OK with who I was when I was young. When I was seventeen years old, in 1945, I started the diary I mentioned earlier. I was exceptionally lonely back then, in part because I felt utterly unattractive. *I'm so short, dumb, and ugly,* I brooded. *If I were normally grown, everything, everything would be much simpler.* Being four foot seven put me so far outside the realm of normal that I was shocked to learn many years later that I was able to become pregnant. I thought carrying a child would be biologically impossible. (After having two children, and now four grandchildren, I'm still overjoyed that my fear was misplaced!)

If you struggle with a disability, loving yourself will be easier if you recognize the obstacles society puts in the way of your efforts to deepen friendships and have sex. If you're a young woman and your friends are getting dressed together before heading to a party, you likely can't join them in the same taxi or Uber if you're confined to a wheelchair. (Or maybe you won't even go because you worry you won't be able to maneuver around the crowd.) Similarly, if you live in a group home, it's likely there are no locks on your door and it's impossible to have the kind of privacy that's conducive to intimacy.

You must accept your reality. Focus instead on what makes you exceptional. Mental and physical differences don't diminish your value. Only after I began to appreciate how smart I was and how advanced I was in school did I recognize that regardless of my height, I was worthy of love. I want the same for you.

Evaluate Your Routine

Self-assessment is critical. If you're not honest with yourself, it's unimaginable that you'll ever make the kinds of life-improving changes you want, no matter if you're longing for more friends or more sex. The more miserable you feel, the greater the need to acknowledge that your own choices are likely contributing to your loneliness.

Let's say you have a stressful job and so every night you turn on your television to find some mind-numbing relaxation. And while you're watching, you forget how lonely you are, and that's a relief. But you're not making friends sitting on your couch. Being passively entertained is a Band-Aid. It's OK, but it will never make loneliness go away.

I know how easy it is to fall into this kind of unhelpful, peopleless trap. After my husband of thirty-five years, Fred Westheimer, passed away, I thought about moving out of the apartment we'd shared for so many decades. I believed that a change of scenery would make me miss him less. But after looking at new places to live, I realized that my feelings of loneliness wouldn't go away just because I was looking at a different set of walls. I'd be missing Fred all the same, just in a different apartment. Slowly I began to understand that a new address would just be another kind of Band-Aid. What I really needed to do was pay greater attention to how I was spending my time. *Instead of apartment hunting, I should be people hunting. I should be inviting friends over or going out for the evening.* People would make me feel better and less alone—not real estate. And they did.

So how do you convince yourself that one or two nights a week you're going to participate in some activity that could lead to making friends or deepening connections instead of watching Netflix? By coming to terms with the seriousness of your situation in relation to loneliness. By paying attention to the times you usually opt to be alone and gradually replacing them with opportunities for social connection. This reckoning must be your motivation for getting out of the house.

Analyze Your Appearance

Note that in the first pages of this section I told you to take a hard look at yourself in the mirror. While the goal there was to make a psychological assessment of how you're doing in the connections-making and connections-keeping departments, while you're at it, give yourself a physical once-over, too.

If you look very lonely—if your hair's a mess, if you always have a frown on your face—it's going to be harder to make new friends. Should you be judged only on your appearance? Of course not, but it's part of human nature to do it anyway, so your first step toward making friends includes looking more approachable.

When I was a young woman, I didn't have a lot of money to buy many new blouses and pants. Plus, for two years I lived on two kibbutzim in Israel, and part of communal living means being more concerned about the welfare of the group than of yourself, including your clothes. But when I started to get noticed in the 1980s, right as my radio program *Sexually Speaking* exploded and I began making television appearances, Pierre Lehu, one of the co-authors of this book and my media director for more than forty years (I call him my minister of communications!), thought it was time for me to pay attention to how strangers were seeing me. I needed to look as kind and pleasant as possible so my advice on using contraception would be easier for people to hear. Pierre would ask me before every live and taped show if I'd gotten my hair done and what I was wearing. I became much more aware of how I presented myself. Every time I got dressed up, I'd call the transformation my "Pierre-ish look."

Consider buying some new clothes. You don't have to spend a lot—going to a thrift or vintage store is a great idea. Select shirts and sweaters that match how you want to feel. Push yourself to choose bright colors. If we deliberately act cheery when we're feeling down, there's a chance we'll actually become happier. The same can be said for the influence clothes and jewelry can have on our mood.

Be Selfish

People are often criticized for taking care of themselves. Or those who do take care of themselves often feel terribly guilty about it. Either way, there are times when you absolutely must put yourself first. (This is true even when you're living on a kibbutz.) And it's perfectly OK to be selfish.

Here's an example.

You have an elderly parent who requires a lot of attention. You've been providing this attention, and because of your ongoing presence, your social life has evaporated and you're feeling lonely. If you're an only child, you may feel stuck and need to come up with a creative solution to give yourself a break. But assuming you have siblings, you must take a stand.

Demand that your siblings help. If they live out of town and that's their built-in excuse for not lending a hand, ask them to send you some money so that you can hire an aide once a week. Use that time to be with friends. If your siblings complain, push back. Loneliness is taking a toll on your life. Explain the sacrifices you've been making. You might even make a list. Detail the errands you're running and the meals you're prepping. Since they don't see all the work you're doing, there's a chance they don't know.

If being overly generous with your time is making you miserable, it's time to be selfish. And let's face it, if your siblings have dumped the entire load of caregiving on your back—the scheduling of doctors' appointments, the overseeing of home repairs—then they've been acting selfishly all along.

Invest in Your Body

You might be shocked to learn, since I am known for talking about sex, that for many years, on and off, my husband Fred and I slept in separate beds. (He snored!) Please don't worry: We found many other places and times to be intimate. But I am a more patient person and generally a much happier person when I get enough rest, and because of that, Fred and I made the joint decision that sleeping apart from time to time was worth it for both of us.

Sleep has always been important to me. One of the hardest aspects of getting back to my normal and busy routine after I had a stroke in 2023, and another minor one this year, was all the trouble I had falling asleep and staying asleep. When it was finally morning and time to begin my day, I was often too tired to do all the talking and planning I wanted to do. I worked with my doctors, changing a few poststroke medications, to get my sleeping routine back on track.

My situation didn't get better immediately, and while that was incredibly frustrating to me, it slowly improved. I was soon able to see friends again, visit with family, and finish writing this book!

I want you to think about how much sleep you're getting. And while you're at it, think about how well you're eating and how much exercise you're getting. If you are not prioritizing rest, if you are not investing in your body, you likely won't have the interest or stamina to engage with other people, and interacting with other people is the only way to create and maintain meaningful connections.

Indulge Yourself

The absence of human touch can be especially painful. Most people crave physical connection—a warm embrace, a thoughtful squeeze on the shoulder—so when we don't have it, we can feel even more isolated. From the moment we are born, skin-to-skin touch contributes to our physical development and mental health. It's been proven to fight disease, help us feel more relaxed, and make us less depressed.

If you're lonely, you may not have the opportunity to be touched very often. One way to counter this vacuum, at least until you develop more intimate relationships, is to treat yourself to manicures, pedicures, and massages. Or get even more creative and go to an acupuncturist. There's no right or wrong number of times to go— indulging every now and then is a chance to feel a sense of physical connection.

When I first hit it big, I bought a massage table and hired a masseuse to come to my apartment once a week. Everyone who worked for me knew I was not available during that time. I was enjoying myself. I was recharging my batteries. I looked forward to being rubbed all over!

By the way, it's possible to enjoy the benefits of massage without spending any money at all. Research at the University of Miami School of Medicine shows that self-massage—rubbing your own arms and legs—also provides positive effects. Why not give it a shot?

Master the Art of Masturbation

Here's a word you might not have expected to find in a book on loneliness, though it may be a little less surprising since it's one of my books: *masturbation*. Being lonely doesn't have to include feeling sexually frustrated.

If you don't have a partner, you should feel free to indulge in some guilt-free masturbation. Be aware, however, that I used the word *some*. As with many other pleasure-inducing activities, too much masturbation—like too many potato chips—can become a problem.

If you're routinely canceling plans so you can stay home to pleasure yourself, that's a warning sign of excessive masturbation. And if you're masturbating every single day, then I say it's likely part of the reason you are lonely.

Frequently reaching climax on your own removes one of the most important incentives for finding a sexual partner. You have to place a limit on how often you engage in this activity. I want your desire for arousal to motivate your search for a healthy sexual relationship. Your longing for intimacy has the capacity to force you out the door, but only if you let it. And that's what I want for you.

Embrace Your Inner Turtle

Making new connections requires courage. If you're shy or lack confidence, if you're an introvert, it can be especially uncomfortable and intimidating to put yourself into social situations. A good remedy for being timid is to embrace your inner turtle.

When a turtle pulls its head and legs inside its shell, it's safe. Nothing can hurt it, but eventually the turtle must stick its neck out. A turtle can't hunt for food, bask in the sun, or find a mate if it plays it safe forever. Turtles must take risks in order to live. The symbolism has always inspired me, and it's why I have an enormous collection of miniature turtles in my apartment. I literally have hundreds. Blue. Yellow. Pink. Red. Rainbow-colored. Green. Most are enameled and covered in rhinestones and imitation gems. They line nearly every one of my bookshelves. There are so many on my living room coffee table, there's no longer room to put my cup of coffee. (Lest you think I've gone off the deep end, most of these turtles were gifts and my collection never seems to stop growing!)

At this point maybe you're assuming, because I have so many turtles, that I never have a problem coming out of my shell. Maybe you're under the impression that it's always been easy for me to talk in front of audiences and deliver speeches. It certainly became easier over the years, especially since I taught sex education in front of hundreds of college students at a time, but I still feel butterflies in my stomach standing in front of a crowd. But I push myself. And you should, too.

I recognize that sometimes even speaking with one person might feel like the scariest stage ever. If that's how it feels to you, if you find yourself frequently staying inside your shell, don't forget to engage your inner turtle. It might help you grow a smidge braver, like it has for me.

Bring a Prop

When my book *Sex for Dummies* was published, the marketing people were very clever with how they promoted the book. They produced keepsake key chains, tiny replicas of the famous bright yellow cover. I don't remember how many I was given to pass out at events, but I am sure I exceeded whatever number they budgeted for. Readers loved them, many asked for extras to give to friends, and I requested more and more to give away.

Looking back, I don't think the key chains were popular simply because they were free. Sure, that was part of it, but I believe people wanted them because they made it easier to approach me. Those little plastic rectangles were conversation starters. Readers who might have been uncomfortable coming up to me otherwise had an easy way to begin talking to me—to ask for a key chain.

Since you probably don't have a key chain with your name on it, how can you make it more likely for someone to walk up to you? What can you do to appear more friendly and open to a conversation?

Think visually.

Put on a T-shirt with the name of your high school or college. Wear a hat with your favorite sport team's logo. Bring a bestselling book to a coffee shop and read it for a while, making sure the cover is visible to anyone who walks by. If you need to get some work done, that's OK. Place a few stickers on your laptop. Choose organizations you support, singers and bands you like, or mountains you've climbed. Welcome any conversations that naturally unfold.

A carefully chosen prop can signal your interests and affiliations. Without saying a word, you've made it easier for like-minded individuals to initiate a conversation with you. And who knows? These shared connections may lead to deeper discussions and potentially the formation of new friendships. (I hope you're realizing by now that I'm urging you to take very small steps in your battle against loneliness. Small steps are important because they're more doable and sustainable than larger ones. Over time, they'll add up and you'll be happier and have more connections!)

Get a Dog

There's no better loneliness-beating pet than a dog. Sure, all pets offer wonders for your psyche. And yes, I do understand cats are cuddly. But for the purposes of this loneliness conversation we're having, animals that you mostly enjoy in solitude won't help you find new human companionship. This is why having a dog is a better option for anyone who is lonely.

Dogs are the most popular pet in the United States, and because of that dogs are people magnets. A dog is your ticket to meet other dog owners at a dog run. A dog is your excuse to go for a walk, multiple times a day, and chat with your neighbors. If you're not comfortable making small talk, dogs can help. A sweet, adorable dog may be just the kind of icebreaker you need!

But let's be clear: Dogs are a lot of work. I wouldn't want you to get one without giving the idea of dog ownership a lot of thought. Learn about the different breeds and what each brings to the table in terms of care and personality. Take into account your own physical abilities. You don't want to get a big and jumpy dog if you're on the frail side. You don't want to get an animal for emotional support only to wind up unable to handle the physical stress and responsibility.

Practice Small Kindnesses

It's a good idea while we're still at the beginning of this book to set the record straight. I've focused so far on the many ways little steps can lead to establishing new and meaningful relationships. But let's pause for a moment. Loneliness is not only about the absence of good friends and sexual partners. Loneliness may stem from not feeling connected much to anyone.

Research shows that if you strike up even the briefest of conversations with a stranger, both of you will feel better and more connected. Asking the person standing next to you in an elevator how their day is going invites conversation. Picking up a piece of mail your neighbor dropped and handing it over with a kind word and a smile sparks discussion. As authors Ryan Jenkins and Steven Van Cohen say in their book *Connectable,* connections don't have to be lasting to be meaningful.

When my daughter, Miriam, was getting married, the best place to shop for wedding dresses was a store in Bay Ridge, Brooklyn, the same New York City neighborhood where Pierre lives. Miriam and I took a car service to the store and looked through every rack for a gown, and then I asked the driver to take us to visit Pierre and his family. I'd never met this driver before, but rather than let him wait in the car for us, I invited him inside. Later, Miriam asked whether the driver was someone I'd hired many times before, but, in fact, it was the first

time. Looking back, we all felt very good meeting someone new that day!

Being comfortable talking with people you don't
know is a skill. It will take time and practice, like getting
better at swimming or playing the piano. I wish there
were a magic button that you could push and—shazam!—
you'd no longer be lonely. Unfortunately there isn't. There
are no shortcuts. But if you make the conscious decision
to interact with strangers, and force yourself to do so regularly, it will enhance feelings of connection to the world
around you. And the more you do it, the easier it will get.

Push Through Rejection

Fear of being rejected is what holds many people back
from making connections. I understand that. Rejection
is hard to take. It makes you sad, angry, and confused,
sometimes all at once. The problem is that rejection is a
part of the human experience. I don't want you to take it
too personally. You can't avoid it, and it's hardly ever
within your control. Certainly, I don't want you to end
your quest for new or deeper relationships because
you're worried about being rejected again. (My guess is
that your luck will change.)

I want you to have only one reaction to rejection:
Lick your wounds and try again. The companions you
make along the way will more than make up for those
who pushed you aside.

Learn the Westheimer Maneuver

One tried-and-true method of meeting new people is to take classes. Now, if your main reason for signing up for a course like painting or Italian cooking is to learn a new hobby, then I'd say sign up for a beginner's class. But since your main goal is to forge new connections, I suggest a different tactic. Yes, sign up for a beginner's class, but pick a course where you already have some expertise!

Why would you do that, you ask? If you're already somewhat skilled, you'll have a leg up on everyone else. If the person next to you is having trouble, you can grin and say, "Here, let me help you with that." Your confidence will soar! And making friends will be so much easier with this newfound well of self-assurance.

I call this approach the Westheimer Maneuver. It's making the decision to be audacious—to do mostly whatever it takes to get what you want. I'll give you an example of how I've put the Westheimer Maneuver into action.

A few years ago, I was about to debate a woman at the Oxford Union, a distinguished debating society in England, about pornography being part of sex education in schools. (I was arguing that porn, if talked about appropriately, should be discussed; she was claiming that it had no place in the classroom.) The Oxford Union is probably the most prestigious site where debates are held, and I was nervous. At the dinner before the event that evening, I noticed that whenever someone proposed a toast, my opponent always took a considerable gulp of wine. I, on the other hand, barely let the wine touch my lips. So I began to chime in. I proposed toast after toast, and the result was that I won the debate easily. You can't be a good debater if you're tipsy!

Taking advantage of circumstances is hardly a new idea. Back in the day, many a lady "accidentally" dropped her handkerchief in front of some man she wanted to meet. Using situations to your advantage, only if it does no harm, isn't trickery—it's chutzpah!

Turn Lemons into Lemonade

My late husband Fred and I met because I refused to accept a less-than-ideal situation. It wasn't a life-or-death predicament, not by a long shot, but I did make an important decision that turned an uncomfortable situation upside down. If I hadn't taken action, my life would be very different today.

Let me tell you what happened.

I've always loved downhill skiing, and one day in 1961 I hit the slopes with three friends because one of them belonged to a ski club and the group had planned a weekend getaway. My ski partner and I were a disaster right from the start. To get to the top of the ski run, we had to use a T-bar—a metal bar skiers put under their tushes to pull them up the mountain. Let me just say that the system works well if two people are similar in height. But for a mismatched pair like us—my friend was more than six feet tall—the mechanism was awkward and difficult to use. When the bar was under *his* tush, it was at my neck; when it was under *my* tush, the bar was at his ankles.

We fumbled and had many false starts. When we finally got to the top, I was so frustrated that I skied off to the side. That's when I spotted Fred. Fred was president of the ski club that my other friend belonged to. Fred was not very tall. Without hesitation, I said to my tall friend: "From now on I'm going up the mountain with that short guy." And that's exactly what Fred and I did.

My decision was abrupt, may even have been rude to my tall friend, but my choice to change ski partners salvaged my day of skiing. It also set me on a new path that opened up other opportunities and possibilities.

There's a saying: When life gives you lemons, make lemonade. If you run into a situation where difficulties make it impossible for you to succeed, don't throw your hands up and cry uncle. Scan your surroundings. Find a solution. Optimists are always more attractive than pessimists. Once you discover a work-around, squeeze your lemon hard and never look back.

Prepare for Conversation

David Letterman had me on his show many times, and I always loved it. On one occasion, the producers came up with a twist: The studio audience would choose nearly everything that unfolded. By the sound of applause, the crowd decided what Dave wore, the theme music to begin the program, and who should read the opening announcements. The routine was hilarious. And then, while the audience was still in a tizzy, Dave asked which of two guests he should bring out first. The choice was between Teri Garr (nominated for an Academy Award for *Tootsie* and one of the stars in Steven Spielberg's *Close Encounters of the Third Kind*) and me. I immediately felt sorry for Teri. Even though she was a lot more attractive than me and a very accomplished actor, my subject matter (sex!) was certain to win the day, and it did.

The lesson here is that when it comes to connecting with people, the ability to be entertaining is key. Have something unusual or provocative to say! Don't be the person who only complains. Don't be the person who always brags about their kids. And never go into a social situation without an idea or two of how you can be interesting.

Pick subjects that are a little off the beaten path yet intriguing to most people. (Stay away from the latest headlines or what's trending on social media, because everyone will probably know about them already.) When there's a lull in conversation, you can break in with "Did you hear . . ." I guarantee you'll have a spot in whatever discussion develops. And be prepared for questions! By digging into your topic just a little bit, you'll be more able to keep the conversation going.

Being curious about people is also a great way to get conversations going. Need suggestions? Here are two from newspaper columnist David Brooks, author of *How to Know a Person: The Art of Seeing Others Deeply and Being Deeply Seen*:

"Where did you grow up?" (Most people enjoy talking about their childhood, so this is a great one!)

"What's your favorite unimportant thing about you?" (David says he likes early Taylor Swift even better than later Taylor Swift. David is known as a serious journalist, so this would be fun to discuss with him at a party!) No matter the questions you ask, he says the goal is the same: to get people talking and telling stories.

And what if you're an introvert? I say practice what you're going to say and give yourself ample time to rest and recharge after you leave any kind of big social event. Introverts aren't necessarily shy, but being in large group settings can be exhausting for them. Instead of drawing energy from people, like I do, introverts tire from external stimulation. If this describes you, know this about yourself and plan time to unwind and regroup after you've gone out for the evening. And while you may not be prepping to go on late-night television, know that everyone who speaks professionally rehearses what they're going to say. So should you.

Don't Hide Who You Are

My first language is German, and I learned Hebrew when I moved to Palestine (before the establishment of Israel) and then French when I lived as a student in Paris. In 1956, when I arrived in the United States, I spoke very little English, and like so many immigrants, I had an accent. My accent identified me as German, and well-meaning friends thought I should take elocution lessons, urging me to modify my accent or get rid of it altogether. (After the war, there was still a lot of anti-German sentiment in New York and other places, and they were concerned for my safety.) But I didn't have the time or money for that, and looking back, I'm glad. My accent is what made me recognizable on the radio. My accent helped make me famous.

If you're an immigrant, I imagine you're trying to fit in as you settle into your new surroundings. But there's no need to go overboard. Don't be ashamed of your accent or your clothing or whatever it is that makes you unique. In fact, use these differences to make friends. When you meet someone new, smile widely and say something like "You understand me despite my accent, right?" This will hopefully start a positive discussion about where you're from and how you got here, and anytime you can start a conversation, you have the opportunity to create a new connection. And if someone clearly doesn't want to be friends with you, no matter the reason, just move on.

And here's one more story about my unique way of talking that you just can't make up: You know what Debra Jo Rupp, the actress who starred in *That '70s Show,* had to do when she played me in Mark St. Germain's play *Becoming Dr. Ruth?* Take lessons on how to speak with *my* accent! How ironic is that?

Travel Wisely

It matters where you sleep when you're on vacation. Yes, I love a big hotel as much as the next person, and my favorite is the King David Hotel in Jerusalem. It has everything I could ever want—a gorgeous outdoor pool, a great view of the city, and plenty of places to sit outside and get a bite to eat. What it doesn't have are ready-made conversation partners. Unless you ask the concierge a question, you could go days without talking with another human being.

This is why I think hostels and especially bed-and-breakfasts are the best accommodations for people who are lonely.

Innkeepers are the perfect hosts. They want to make you feel at home because in most cases where you're staying is their home. Without your having to ask a question, owners recommend what to do and what to see during your visit. And for breakfast, instead of seating you in a cavernous room where guests tend to stick to themselves, they'll show you to a table in a small space with very few other guests, where conversations are far more likely to happen. Perhaps you'll decide to check out the local museum with another solo traveler.

Choose Mental Wealth

I grew up in Frankfurt. Before the Nazis came to power, it was a wonderful place to be a child. My neighborhood was idyllic. It seemed that I knew every neighbor and that my parents always had an extra pair of hands to take me to the store or walk me to school.

For some people, especially those in the United States who are college-educated, it's common these days to move a great distance because of work. A new job across the country might offer a better job title and salary. But uprooting yourself from childhood friends and family comes at a cost.

What happens if you decide a decade or so after you

move to start a family? If you're three thousand miles away from your parents, you won't have that ready-made support system. You might feel increasingly alone and isolated. The same would be true if you needed ongoing help after breaking your leg or managing a chronic illness. When life is hard, it might be easier if you're surrounded by people who've known and loved you for a lifetime. (It will also be easier to care for aging parents—and feel more connected to them—if you don't live in a different time zone.)

I urge you to prioritize your mental (not just financial) wealth. Yes, I know that money is important and that I am writing from a place where I haven't struggled to pay my bills for a long time, but try not to make work the only factor when considering where to live. My advice is to think about how your everyday existence might look years from now when your lifestyle and needs change.

Communicate Your Needs

You should always tell people what you need, and that's especially true if you're grieving. Loneliness increases when you feel the people closest to you aren't supporting you or don't understand what you're going through. But let's not assume the worst of them. They may have zero experience with loss, and they're certainly not mind readers. Unless you tell people how they can show up for you, how should they know?

My co-author Allison is a journalist, and she writes a lot about grief. If you're feeling alone because nobody remembered to call you on the anniversary of your loved one's death, Allison advises that you ask at least one person to mark the date on their calendar so that *next year* you're assured a phone call.

I've always told my radio listeners and TV watchers to communicate their wishes in the bedroom. If you like to be stimulated a certain way, you need to tell your lover what to do! If you like oral sex, you should ask your partner for more oral sex! This kind of directness is important at all times in your life, and that includes times of great sadness. Communicating your needs will help your needs be met, and when your needs are met, you will feel less lonely. This is uniquely true when dealing with family, and that's precisely why we're going to focus on family relationships next.

Family

FAMILY PLAYS AN ESSENTIAL ROLE IN REDUCING loneliness. When relationships are possible, family members provide a unique and powerful sense of belonging and understanding. They also contribute a feeling of security, a go-to support system, so much so that it's possible you might never experience the sensation of being completely alone. And because family relationships are so vital for social connection, doing whatever you can to preserve, repair, and strengthen these bonds should be a priority.

Of course, not all family situations are positive, I realize, and I recognize that the absence of family connections can feel incredibly isolating. You likely grew up with the understanding that family is supposed to have your back no matter what—so that when you no longer have access to that kind of unconditional love and support, you may feel particularly empty. I also know, because I lost my family so young, that death can be a significant cause of loneliness. I tried to stay in touch with my family after we were separated. We wrote letters back and forth for a time, but then my letters stopped being answered. I longed for family so much and for so long that I eventually built myself a new one from scratch.

This portion of the Menu for Connection is about rebuilding connections with family—whether you're estranged, separated by loss, or just living far away.

The American Psychological Association defines loneliness as "discomfort or uneasiness from being or perceiving oneself to be alone." Pay close attention to just one of these words: *perceiving*.

How lonely you feel depends on how you *perceive* your circumstances. If you think you are powerless, then you are likely going to feel worse. But here I am. I'm telling you that it's possible to mend relationships with parents and siblings, build an entirely new family when your birth family no longer exists, rekindle a relationship with an estranged family member, and even maintain close relationships with family members who are no longer alive. (In cases of physical and mental abuse, it may be safest and more empowering to focus on creating new family-type connections instead.)

Follow my advice. When you put effort into strengthening family connections, your life can change. It can become richer and fuller. My bet is that you'll also be happier.

Rethink Your Thinking

If you're lucky, family offers a safe harbor from the world. You feel accepted into the group, like you belong, no matter what. Shared history, traditions, and values create this kind of powerful connection. And yet family can easily be torn apart. And not just by what we say or do but also by how we think. I am sure you know that our mind, in many ways, controls our actions. Negative thinking often brings more negativity into our lives. Positive thinking, you guessed it, frequently brings more positivity into our lives.

I believe you can mend nearly any hurt just by changing the way you think. Mind over matter. Even if we can't change our circumstances (maybe you and your family member are no longer speaking to each other), we can change the way we view those circumstances. Pushing ourselves to believe that one day we'll see a brighter tomorrow opens us up to the possibility that life won't always be so bleak and that we'll be able to repair nearly any family relationship.

I learned this lesson when I was ten years old.

When my father was taken away by the Nazis, I was in our apartment in Frankfurt. I remember watching from the window as he was led into a truck. He looked up at me and smiled. I've never forgotten the reassuring expression on his face. I'm sure he wasn't in the mood to smile. He must have feared what might happen to him next, what would happen to me, his only child. But his decision to smile in that dreadful moment made me hopeful.

When my mother and grandmother put me on a train to Switzerland a few weeks later, part of the Kindertransport to save the lives of Jewish children, I made sure my grandmother and mother saw me smiling out the window when the train left the station. I was terrified and had no idea if I would ever see my parents and grandmother again, but I did what I could to make them feel better, just as my father had done for me.

Sometime on the journey, as improbable as it sounds, I stood on my seat and started to sing the Hebrew songs we all were taught in school. I sang as loudly as I could. The other children soon joined me, and for the rest of the ride, there was no crying, only singing.

To patch relationships with family members, you might need to fake a smile until a real smile emerges. You might need to forgive or forget. And you might need to change your mindset—to believe that a relationship is fixable and not broken forever. You'll be more likely to rebuild fractured relationships because you'll be pushing yourself to look at bad situations with a little more optimism.

By the way, I learned something else on that train. I began to understand how wonderful it feels to make others feel better. I have no idea if I made my mother and grandmother feel better when they saw me smile out the window, but I was trying to give them hope, like my father had given me. And while I didn't have any family with me on that train, I did have one companion: my favorite doll. There was a little girl half my age sitting next to me. She was crying even harder than I was. So what did I do? I gave her my doll. These were the germs of my becoming a therapist, of my realizing I had the power to make people feel better.

Go to Gatherings

Push yourself to attend weddings, graduations, confirmations, quinceañeras—any gathering where family is involved. Don't allow your distaste for any one aunt or uncle, niece or nephew, to keep you away. The lonelier you are, the more you need your family. If you hide yourself away every time your family assembles, you're cutting yourself off from building on the relationships you do enjoy. But the scenario can also play out much worse than this.

If you always skip family events, if you always come up with some excuse for why it isn't possible for you to go, pretty soon they'll begin to write you off and you won't be invited at all. You may end up with no baby showers and no retirement parties to celebrate.

Yes, I know it can be unpleasant to have to grin while some relative fills your ear with comments you despise. But keep in mind that family events are social events, and you can move around as if you're at a cocktail party—moving from one conversation to the next, not spending too long with anyone.

Be Less Judgmental

Everyone experiences loneliness, but because you are reading this book, it seems you are maybe feeling lonelier than most. This is a clue that you're not perfect. You, like the rest of us, have flaws.

Why do I bring this up?

Because undoubtedly you have family members who also have imperfections. Are they annoying because they talk incessantly? Do they irritate you because they think they're smarter than you? Whatever your grievance, since you also are not perfect, and because you're feeling disconnected, you have to find a way to make peace with them and fold them into your life.

Ignore what irks you. Bite your tongue. Hold your breath. Suck on a mint. Drink tea. Or make a decision to lean into it and adapt—instead of throwing away the relationship.

If your aunt always goes on and on about the same topic, the next time you see her, come prepared with questions about another subject so you can redirect the conversation. If your grandmother can't hear very well and you hate having to shout, make a point of not talking so much and simply hold her hand. I promise you she'll like it, and you'll both feel less lonely.

By the way, I'm not shy about asking friends and relatives to hold my hand. It's a way of communicating that works for me no matter how sad, frustrated, or tired I might feel. Touch is powerful. Without saying a word, it can help us feel less alone.

Admit Your Mistakes

In late 1985 and early 1986, I was caught up in a rather large controversy. It began when a librarian in Ramsey, New Jersey, reached out to my publisher to complain about my book *First Love*. She told my editor that, effective immediately, it was being removed from circulation. No, the book wasn't being banned. It wasn't too explicit. The problem was a small yet significant typo.

In a passage about reducing the risk of pregnancy, I wrote that it's safe to have sex the week before and the week of ovulation. But that's incorrect. The word *safe* should have been *unsafe*. The publisher recalled 115,000 copies of the book, we added those two all-important letters, and it was rereleased with an entirely new cover. I don't know how that mistake wound up in the book, as I certainly knew the correct information, but I didn't hesitate to take full responsibility. My name was on the book, so it was my fault.

How are you at admitting your mistakes? Your refusal to say "I'm sorry" could be one of the reasons your family relationships have suffered. It might also be one of the reasons you're lonely. To resuscitate these connections, you may need to swallow your pride. You may need to extend that apology, even if it should have been offered years ago. When you acknowledge wrongdoing, you are better positioned to get family relationships back on track.

Even if your fumbles don't make national headlines (my error was covered by nearly every newspaper and magazine in America), it's never too late to make things right. Keep your ego in check. Don't let it cause any more distance and pain.

Channel Your Inner Shark

Having thick skin is important for keeping and nurturing family relationships because if you can't take a joke, if your feathers get ruffled too easily, you might as well decide that being lonely isn't so bad after all. You might have a rude stepfather. Your mother's politics may offend you. You have to learn to look the other way. You have to develop the thickest skin of anyone you know. The whale shark has one of the thickest skins of any animal in the world. To keep family connections close, you must channel your inner shark!

I kept my mouth shut plenty of times with Fred's relatives. Some were less than thrilled when he told them we were getting married. I was not the catch they were hoping for. I was a single mother, and they didn't think I was good enough for him. From the moment Fred reported this back to me, I had to smile and be friendly whenever I saw them, all the while knowing they were against our marriage. Over the years, my attitude toward them softened. They were loving toward me, and I adored them. If I had held on to my anger, we all would have missed out.

If someone is inconsiderate, let it go. If it happens again and again, address the problem directly. Make sure tension doesn't build and emotional wounds don't fester. And if you learn family members are talking about you behind your back, it might be best to think about whale sharks and just keep your lips closed.

Be a Good Listener

I mentioned on page 28 that when I first stepped foot in the United States I barely spoke English. I knew how to exchange a few pleasantries, but as a refugee, I found it challenging to navigate New York and start over again. My lifeline was a German Jewish newspaper called the *Aufbau*. Reading the paper one day, I spotted an ad that would change my life: The New School of Social Research was offering a scholarship for a master's degree in sociology. Only victims of the Nazis could apply. The next day I went to the school, and twenty-four hours later I got the scholarship. The New School is where I met Hannah Strauss, who quickly became my best friend.

Hannah—more than anyone else before or since—taught me one of the most valuable lessons in maintaining deep connections: Be a good listener. Hannah seemed to appreciate whatever I had to say. Whenever we talked, I felt like all of her attention was on me. She never brushed aside my troubles, and she always wanted to hear my good news. By actively listening, by giving me her unrushed and undivided focus, Hannah made me feel important, and that good feeling made me like her even more. When I became a therapist, I tried my best to copy Hannah's way of being. In my private practice, I wanted to be the best listener I could be and help my clients arrive at their own solutions. On my radio show, I wanted callers to know that their concerns were valid and that I wouldn't judge them for asking a question.

When you listen, you can't talk, and when you don't talk, you can't come across as a know-it-all. You also can't make people feel stupid for their indecision or actions. Family members will feel closer to you, and your relationships will deepen, when you acknowledge their worries but don't chime in every chance you get with your opinions. Sit with your child's problems and don't be ready to fix them so quickly.

Families often experience rifts when there's too much talking and not enough listening. The next time you want to offer some unsolicited advice, I hope you'll think about Hannah. Open your ears and close your mouth as much as possible.

Be Vulnerable

I come from a long line of German Jews who don't typically complain. My family always thought it best to be stoic. And while to some extent I remain this way, it's no longer possible to completely keep my problems to myself. Today, because of my age, I've come to accept there are some challenges that I can't solve on my own. I tell my daughter, Miriam, and my son, Joel, everything that involves my healthcare, and they make sure I have the help I need to safely navigate my apartment. It wasn't easy admitting that I needed help. It wasn't in my nature to accept assistance or show weakness. In many ways, looking back on my life now, I should have leaned on others more frequently than I did. Doing so certainly would have made being a young working mother easier.

I want you to learn from my experiences and ask for more support. Please don't take this to mean that I advocate hanging a sign around your neck that declares "I'm lonely" and walking around your neighborhood. What I want you to do is appoint your own personal ambassador to loneliness. Reach out to at least one family member and tell that one person the truth about how you're feeling. Perhaps a cousin, aunt, or grandparent can play this role. Confide in that one person. Give your ambassador permission to tell others in your family that you'd welcome more texts, phone calls, and visits.

Loneliness is invisible. You might put on such a

good front that nobody in your family is even aware that you're lonely. If you don't admit you need help, help may never come.

Say Their Name Out Loud

There are many reasons why families no longer talk about one family member or another. Death. Prison. Divorce. Drugs. Estrangement for any reason. Abuse of any kind. While you can't bring a loved one back from the dead, and you can't unilaterally shift perceptions of the black sheep of the family, you can determine what you do and what you say in any given situation.

Tell stories about your sister, brother, mother, or father—even if no one else does. Bring their name up in conversation. You can be the one person in your family who acknowledges a birthday or the anniversary of a death.

Ignoring that there was an important person in your family and feeling that you're the only person who still remembers or cares can make you feel especially alone and disconnected. That's loneliness on top of loneliness—you're missing your loved one and you're not able to talk about your loved one. To beat back loneliness, say the name of your missing family member out loud. Do this whenever the moment moves you, at any time you crave a sense of connection.

Fabricate an Excuse

If you no longer speak with members of your family simply because too much time has passed, you might benefit from creating an excuse to get back in touch. Sure, you could just start by calling cousins out of the blue, but that might feel awkward. A perfectly acceptable reason to get back in touch is to get their help with a genealogy project. If you're not researching your family tree or writing up your family's history, it's time to get started. Get started right now!

Your first phone call is simply to invite them to lend a hand. If relatives happen to live nearby, make a point of saying, "Let's make a plan to look at photographs together." Of course, if meeting one-on-one feels strange, you could try to piece together a small group of relatives instead. A gathering would allow everyone to share memories, and I bet each person who participates will feel a surge of meaningful connection, most of all *you*—since you're the one who did all the planning to make it happen.

If creating a video is more your style, you could ask relatives to sit down with you for interviews. I've made several documentaries, two as a producer and one that I starred in called *Ask Dr. Ruth,* by the director Ryan White. You may not see yourself as a documentary filmmaker, but I suggest you begin rethinking that. Working on a film is fun. It also has the capacity to bring family back into your life. But no matter what kind of genealogy project you choose, a shared endeavor is a perfect way to mend or rekindle familial relationships.

Have Family Game Night

Even if you have a great relationship with your spouse and children, the everyday demands of raising a family can make you feel more like a short-order cook than a parent who is seen, valued, and loved. Feeling unnoticed and unappreciated is not a good recipe for feeling connected to family. In fact, a root cause of loneliness is being surrounded by people who you expect will make you feel whole but instead make you feel like part of the furniture.

Family game nights can help. For a few hours, the whole family can play with one another and not worry about chores, to-do lists, or homework. Children see their parents as playmates, not taskmasters. Remembering to take time out to play can make everyone feel closer and more connected.

When I started to become more famous, I was asked to endorse many products. I rejected most of these offers, because the advice I was giving was important and I didn't want people to think I was some sort of huckster. I wanted to be known as a trained expert, and I wanted my advice to be trusted. But I did agree to having one board game with my name on it—Dr. Ruth's Game of Good Sex. I considered it a great way to deliver valuable sex education to an even wider audience. And while I would never recommend it for family game night (it's not at all appropriate for children!), I do suggest competing against one another with games like Apples to Apples and Ticket to Ride or classics like Clue or the great card game euchre.

In an unexpected way, working on Dr. Ruth's Game of Good Sex made me feel closer to my parents. When the venture was just taking off, I needed to pick a name for my company. I chose Karola Inc. in recognition of my birth name, Karola. When I immigrated to Israel, I was told Karola sounded too German and that I should change it. I decided to flip my first and middle names. My middle name, Ruth, became my first name. My first name, Karola, became my middle name.

I had been fearful of getting rid of Karola altogether. If there was any chance my mother and father had survived the concentration camps and were looking for me, I needed them to see Karola associated with my name. Sadly, even though my dream never came true, looking back now, choosing to name my company Karola Inc. strengthened my relationship with them. It renewed my sense of connection to my parents.

Share the Fun

I've always loved playing chess. As soon as my grandchildren were old enough, I took out my chessboard and we'd compete. Pitting your wits against one another—no matter the game you choose—is a fantastic bonding opportunity. And before you argue, "But my grandchildren live too far away," you can still play games even if they live in another state or country.

The New York Times is my favorite newspaper and has some of the best games for nurturing family relationships. Wordle, Connections, and The Mini Crossword are all great ones to try. What's terrific about them is that everyone plays the same game on the same day— offering a consistent way to stay in touch no matter the distance. And because players can easily share their results with one another via text, I know many parents who play with their college-age kids, too. For them, it's an easy and enjoyable way to stay in touch throughout the academic year.

Sharing scores and bragging rights isn't serious— but the benefits of all that reliable social interaction are. After all, maintaining connections is easier when we can share experiences.

Lose Count

When Miriam was a baby and I was a single mother, I had no money for a babysitter in order to go out with family or friends. My solution was to throw parties in my apartment. The remedy was so simple and successful that I continued to host gatherings in my living room long after Miriam was an adult. Larry Angelo, my wonderful cohost on Lifetime's *Good Sex, with Dr. Ruth Westheimer* and other TV shows, remembers them well. "Everyone brought things to eat and drink and you'd call them 'Bring Something' parties," he fondly recalled as we reminisced for this book. Time and time again I'd offer up my home. I made myself a perpetual hostess.

If you're always the one initiating plans, whether to organize a small gathering or a large family reunion, it's easy to get resentful and say "Enough." I understand the desire to count how many times your invitations go unreciprocated. But I encourage you to change your thinking: Your payback isn't a future dinner at your relative's house. Your payback is having the opportunity to strengthen your connections right now, on your own timetable.

We can never understand what's going on behind a relative's closed doors. Maybe your cousin is self-conscious about her home. Perhaps the expense of hosting (providing drinks and anything else) feels a bit too much. At the end of the day, decide to be a host because it makes you feel less isolated. Don't even think about being invited anywhere ever. Try to focus on the upside—having relatives to spend time with and enjoying their company.

Be a Team Player—Literally

In my therapy practice, I saw clients with many different kinds of sexual problems. Couples who lost interest in sex were very common. What was also common was *why* they had lost interest in sex. Frequently they had fallen into a pattern of feeling disconnected from each other. Even though they were living under the same roof, going to sleep and waking up in the same bed, they felt lonely. Perhaps lonelier than if they were single, because they had unmet expectations of feeling close and connected.

To get back on track, think outside the bedroom and consider what fun activities you could do with your partner. Relationships frequently suffer when couples stop doing stuff together. Pickleball is typically played in pairs. Two people are on each side of the net at all times. I love the idea of you and your partner forming a team together. I also happen to love dancing. Dancing—in particular ballroom, salsa, foxtrot, and more—requires that you rely on your partner and operate in unison. It also demands plenty of touching, always a good thing for couples!

Physical activity has the power to rebuild emotional intimacy. When you play a sport together, you must work collaboratively to win. When you dance, you have to clasp hands and thrust your pelvis into your partner's hips. Physical closeness and synchronized movement have the power to enhance emotional bonds. They also create shared memories, enabling couples to deepen their connection even further.

Grow Independently

Please don't take my previous point to mean that you have to spend every free second with your partner to feel connected. The secret is finding a healthy blend of time together and time apart. Somewhere in the middle is where you will feel full and complete. Somewhere in the middle is where you'll recognize yourself and feel like you belong in your own home.

When I married Fred, my third husband, he already had a paramour: a plot of land he owned on Lake Oscawana in Putnam Valley, New York. He loved nothing more than spending time there—with or without me. The kids and I enjoyed the water, but if I had something else to do (and my travel schedule was quite hectic for years), I'd routinely take a pass. But truthfully, that didn't upset him. He was more than happy to go alone. If he'd been stuck in our Washington Heights apartment with no companion, I'm sure he would have resented my going off all the time. And if I had put my work on the back burner just to accommodate him, I would have felt angry and diminished.

Going in different directions can fortify relationships. Once we shelve what's most important to us, once we start making so many compromises we lose our sense of self, that's when loneliness bubbles up. Don't accept a bad situation. Talk it out with your spouse or partner. There's more to life than wallowing in misery.

Set a New Course

If your misery is unshakable no matter how many activities you try with and without your partner, you might be better off ending your relationship and starting fresh. Believe me, I know what I'm talking about. I've been in three marriages. I mentioned already that my beloved Fred was my third husband. What I haven't told you yet is anything about the other two.

David (pronounced Dah-VEED) was my first husband. We met through mutual friends when I was teaching kindergarten in Israel. He was smart and handsome. Even better, he was short and a good dancer! I fell for David immediately and we were engaged and married all within a few months.

What a mess it turned out to be. We married too young and grew apart.

I met Dan after David. By this time, I was living in Paris, and we decided to leave France and head to the United States. We weren't married, but when we arrived in New York, we found an apartment together through that newspaper I told you about, the *Aufbau*. Then I got pregnant by accident. And then we got married. Miriam was born one year after I arrived in America, but even Miriam, this gorgeous and perfect baby, couldn't make our marriage last.

Dan and I realized we weren't right for each other. As with my marriage to David, if Dan and I had forced ourselves to stay together, I would have been miserable and lonely. He wasn't the right partner for me, and he would never become the right partner, even if we had spent eternity side by side.

Have you and your partner drifted in different directions, too? Might counseling repair your relationship? Possibly. Therapists aren't magicians, though, and if a relationship needs to end, the sooner you make the split the better. And even though personal finances may make some situations more complicated than others, my hope is that you'll find your way to another partner—one who will make you feel happier and more complete. As long as your spirit is free to soar, you'll have the freedom to get to know yourself again and develop a new and far more fulfilling romantic relationship.

Preserve In-law Relationships

Dan didn't have family, but David did, and after David and I divorced, I made sure to stay in touch. As you know, I lost my mother, father, and grandparents during the Holocaust, and other than one uncle who lived in California, I had no family whatsoever before I gave birth to Miriam. I wasn't keen on losing David's family, too. I happily remained in contact with his father for years.

Some people make the mistake of losing half their family when they get divorced. This can also happen when a spouse dies. Going your separate ways may be unavoidable after a bitter divorce, but many marriages don't end dramatically. All it takes is some effort on your part and you will likely be able to keep those in-law relationships going. And certainly if your spouse has died, it might be possible to reach out to your in-laws to stay involved in their lives. Don't cast aside a pool of companions who already know you and loved you.

How might you do this? On birthdays, make a phone call. Chat for a while. If possible, make a date to see your former mother-in-law or father-in-law in person. If everyone in that extended family exchanges holiday presents, keep up the tradition. Any demonstration of goodwill will help maintain or rebuild these crucial relationships.

Stay Connected to Loved Ones

The oldest object I own is a washcloth. Besides a few photographs of my parents and grandparents, it's the only possession I have from my childhood. Even though there's a pocket for my hand and it would be quite useful when I take a shower or bath, I never get it wet. It's more of a museum piece. I keep it inside a sealed plastic storage bag so I can look at it but don't have to worry about getting it dirty or stained.

I took the washcloth with me the day I left Germany and boarded that train to Switzerland. I packed it in my bag when I left Switzerland for Israel, and I made sure it was in my suitcase when I left Israel for France and later the United States. I am ninety-six years old and I left Frankfurt when I was ten. And while a few of the white and navy-blue threads are pulled and frayed, most of the orange and yellow ones are in good condition, a miracle of sorts to me. I feel objects can convey the relationship you had with loved ones. The washcloth is a reminder of my parents. It helps me feel connected to them.

Family members who are deceased can still be part of your life. Just because they are not physically present doesn't mean their presence can't make you feel less alone. There's a book from the nineties called *Continuing Bonds* that's gained considerable appreciation among therapists for its ideas about connecting with loved ones who've died. The authors argue that our "devotion and affection do not end with a death," and because of that, the bereaved don't need to sever ties with the person they loved; instead, they can continue their relationship through "dreams, memories, conversations about them, and cherished objects that remind us of them."

I also think you can talk to your loved ones.

If your mother died when you were an adult, and assuming you had a good relationship, when you think of a question you wish she were alive to answer, your mind will likely come up with the kind of response she might have offered. You knew her well. Your subconscious is able to paint a vivid picture of what an actual conversation with her might be like right now. And while I wouldn't want you to spend all day talking to your dead mother, if you do it from time to time and these visits help relieve your loneliness, then they're something that you should turn to whenever you need to feel a sense of connection. Don't be alarmed if you get emotional. That's OK and not unusual.

I must tell you one more thing about my washcloth and why it remains so special to me. It's embroidered with my initials, K.S.—for Karola Siegel—in cranberry-red thread. The letters aren't visible from the outside. They're tucked inside the mouth, where your wrist would touch if it were on your hand. The only way to see the stitching is to pick up the washcloth and look inside. And when I do put my hand inside, I'm transported back to Frankfurt and being around my family.

Give Yourself a Break

We all do a good job beating ourselves up. Maybe you've caused your parents, siblings, or children a lot of pain. Shame and guilt may be the reasons you are lonely.

Cut yourself some slack right now.

No matter what you've done, no matter whom you've hurt, don't lock yourself in a fortress of your own making. If you need to make amends, do it. Take steps, no matter how big or small, to repair the damage you've caused. Begin the healing process so you can open yourself up to connections, not close yourself off.

Everyone is worthy of close relationships. Tell anyone in your family who asks that Dr. Ruth says so.

Seek New Family

If for some reason you don't have family, take it from me: You can build a new one. Weaving a family of your own choosing can alleviate loneliness. It doesn't matter why you no longer have family. Maybe, as was the case with me, they've all died. Or perhaps, because of work, they no longer live close by. Does any of this mean you no longer have family to spend time with? Does this mean you have zero support when you need it? My answer is always the same: Absolutely not!

Throughout my life, people who were willing to be close friends, not just acquaintances, were swept up into my definition of family. I could rely on them and they could rely on me. It didn't matter if they lived down the block or on another continent. I put the same energy into maintaining contact with these friends as most people put into staying in touch with their own relatives. I established a new family unit because I longed for that sense of security and unconditional love, the kind you get from family.

What could this look like for you in practice?

Let's say you have friends who live far away. You

haven't been in touch for an extended period of time, so it might feel uncomfortable reaching out. Get over that discomfort! No matter the distance, no matter how long it's been since you've talked, I want you to commit to getting back in touch—and staying in touch.

If your goal is to turn your friendships into family relationships, you have to be proactive. Some friends may be resistant to increasing their involvement in your life, but I imagine most will welcome the opportunity. They'll want to spend more time with you and know you even better. Naturally, to create a family out of your friendships, you need a few good friends in the first place. In the next section, I'll explore exactly how to find them.

Friends and Lovers

VERY SINGLE PERSON ON THIS GREAT BIG PLANET of ours could potentially become a friend or lover. I'm aware this is an overstatement and also probably a little overwhelming, but my goal is to give you hope. Say to yourself over and over again until you believe it: *I am going to make new friends. I am going to find a romantic partner.*

If after repeating these words you're still convinced that you'd need a miracle to change your predicament, know that miracles happen, because to some degree my life has been full of them. But you must never passively wait around for divine intervention or inexplicable good fortune. Friends and lovers generally don't show up one day unannounced. Relationships that matter need to be cultivated.

Finding the just-right friend or romantic partner requires a lot of dating. In many ways, building meaningful connections is a numbers game. You could meet someone and spend a lot of time together, and then, for whatever reason, the relationship fizzles. I suggest bettering your odds by planting many seeds and seeing which ones blossom. Every idea in this "Friends and Lovers" chapter will help.

I've been saying throughout this book that the solution to loneliness is in your hands. Curing loneliness won't happen immediately; it is a deliberate, step-by-step process. Like a farmer, you have to put work into that connections field of yours if you expect it to yield any produce. Coming to terms with this notion will make finding your way less burdensome. It's only if you lock yourself away and do nothing that you're bound to continue feeling disconnected and alone.

The strategies below will guide you in nurturing the kinds of friendships you are seeking—ones that bring you comfort and fulfillment and, when it comes to romance, lots of great sex. And don't discount a miracle or two happening along the way! As long as you're moving in the right direction, there's no telling what might happen.

Broaden Your Friendcabulary

The word *friend* has many meanings. There are casual friends, work friends, friends of friends, best friends forever, childhood friends, fair-weather friends, and friends with benefits. Don't get caught up in the idea that if you don't have a single best friend, you're doomed. I am a strong believer that there are many types of worthwhile friendships, and developing all kinds will make you feel less isolated.

In my life, I've had many types of friends, and each offers me something special. There's my oldest friend and first boyfriend, Putz (pronounced Pootz, unlike the Yiddish insult). We haven't been a thing in decades, and he lives in Israel, but I still feel a deep and satisfying connection to him every time we talk, and he still calls me Karola. And then there's Cliff, whom I met almost forty years ago at the height of Dr. Ruth mania. He had just graduated from college, and I needed help managing my office, in particular the thousands of fan letters I received every week. We formed such a close bond that I brought him along as a personal assistant, then a production assistant, when I launched my nationally syndicated *Ask Dr. Ruth* TV show. Fast-forward four decades, and he usually visits me once a week, at other times we talk on the phone, and because he's in a band, I've gone to see him perform many times.

Another terrific friend is Erik. He's a relatively new friend. Erik lives in my apartment building and we're able to see each other nearly every day, often twice a day. We're collaborating on a musical project that will help bring grandparents and grandchildren together. (You can learn more about the concert we're creating in the September section of "Your Monthly Calendar.")

You might notice that all the ones I mentioned are men. I certainly have many good friends who are women, but I wanted to make a point. You can be friends with anyone, male or female, straight or gay. Don't cut off anyone because you have the idea that a friend must have the same anatomy or sexual orientation as you.

It might be wonderful to have a BFF, but having one is not necessary for living a full and connected life. Don't get hung up on the idea that you need to find a best buddy right away. Right now, I just want you to seek individuals to spend time with and then take your time building rewarding connections with those who seem the most promising.

Curate Your Social Circle

You must be the boss of your social life. When you're decisive about whom you spend time with, when you exercise agency in your relationships, you're better able to nurture the kinds of connections that are built on shared values and interests and bring you joy. If you're keeping people around out of laziness, habit, or inertia— and not because they're genuinely interested in you or make you feel good about yourself—you need to take stock of your connections and make some changes. Your well-being depends on it.

Everyone who knows me well knows that I hate complaining. People who spend too much time grumbling are less capable of offering you positive relationships. My advice is to surround yourself with people who are fully invested in living. Avoid people who whine all the time. They won't lift you up, and they certainly won't expand your world in the way you're hoping for.

This is not an all-or-nothing proposition. There's no need to cut people out of your life entirely, especially if they offer you even a small measure of happiness. Instead, take small steps to grow your circle with purpose. Then, gradually, begin spending more time with these more positive and optimistic people.

Don't Judge a Book by Its Cover

There's no doubt you'll meet someone someday who doesn't seem, at least at first, like a good friend or long-term partner candidate. Try not to judge a book by its cover. If you make a rash decision, you might be cutting yourself off from a connection before it has the chance to start.

I came very close to losing a major opportunity because I was too quick to dismiss it. I was traveling overseas—I don't remember exactly where I was—when Pierre called to say that the publisher of the Dummies books wanted me to write *Sex for Dummies*. I wasn't familiar with the series, so I said, "Tell them no. I don't write books for dummies." But Pierre didn't listen to me. He informed the publisher that he couldn't reach me. He knew I was making a big mistake. When I returned to New York, Pierre convinced me to go to a bookstore and look at some Dummies books. After seeing them, I changed my mind. *Sex for Dummies* sold hundreds of thousands of copies and was translated into seventeen languages.

I admit that when I heard *dummies,* I reacted only to that one word. I was wrong. In your case, don't let snap judgments ruin your chances of developing a good and satisfying relationship. You can build deep connections with people who have different political views and religious beliefs. I bet someone you didn't initially think was attractive may actually grow on you!

First impressions might tell you everything you need to know, but not always. Push yourself to give people a second or third chance. If you do, you might discover someone worth befriending.

Organize Concrete Plans

If you're longing to get out of your house to be with another person, don't be satisfied with superficial, nonspecific phone calls and texts. Checking in to say hello or find out the latest news is an important way to stay active in each other's lives, but you know what's missing from that kind of back-and-forth? Making an actual date to see each other!

The next time you text or call a friend, be the one who suggests a date, time, and place to get together in person. It's better to be proactive than passive. By taking control of the situation, you're more likely to get what you want—a potential partner to have dinner with or a friend who will join you for a walk around the block.

And if they say, "Great idea! I'll get back to you," and then they don't, make certain you call or text them back. Be a little pushy. They might not need to socialize as much as you do, which is why you're the one who needs to do the suggesting. You know what I do? When I say goodbye to a dear friend, I always ask, "When will I see you again?" The question delays our departure by a few minutes, but nobody cares. We get out our calendars (I still use a paper one!) and happily mark another date to see each other.

Set Aside Time

Creating meaningful connections requires work. If it were easy, I doubt the U.S. surgeon general would have felt the urgency to declare loneliness an epidemic. As I said in "Self," you must evaluate your routine and make it a priority. But it will take time.

One pioneering study by Dr. Jeffrey Hall, director of the Relationships and Technology Lab at the University of Kansas, shows that it takes about twelve thousand minutes to develop a new best friend. He also found that it takes at least 120 hours over the first three weeks to develop a good friendship, and more than 200 hours over six weeks to turn a friend into a best friend.

I don't bring this study up, though, to obsess about how many minutes it takes to make a friend. You already know it takes substantial effort. The point I want you to focus on, in addition to the amount of time you're devoting to your social life, is what else Dr. Hall discovered: He determined that it matters what you *do* during that time. You could be in the same book club for years, seeing the same people over and over again, but if you do nothing to advance those relationships, those individuals will remain acquaintances and nothing more. So what to do? For starters, I hope you're already trying out some of the strategies in this book, like being approachable and actively listening. But to supercharge your connections, you must also pay attention to context.

Pay Attention to Context

The spark that drives all kinds of relationships forward is doing activities together. The reason for this is not complicated. Making the choice to have fun together—or deciding to carve out a few moments to have a private discussion—communicates interest, not obligation, and the communication of mutual interest is essential for turning acquaintances into deeper connections.

A friend of mine has a box for the opening night of

the U.S. Open tennis matches. I used to be a regular guest, and so was President Bill Clinton. We'd sit aside from the others and talk and talk, but not about the points or players. Sure, getting those free tickets put us in the same place at the same time, but our physical proximity is not the reason our long-time friendship grew. It grew because we made the choice to break away from the group and concentrate on each other.

Sharing experiences creates opportunities to appreciate people and see them in a new light. It also creates time to nurture relationships.

Talk Openly

You might get to know someone incrementally by joking around, but to strengthen relationships, you must share updates about your life and have meaningful discussions. The best conversations might make you feel uncomfortable, especially at first, but don't give up. (Remember the first time you had sex? Losing your virginity might not have been the best experience, but I am hoping you've had lots of great sex and orgasms since.) Talking openly might feel a bit similar. Just follow my advice. As with good sex, you'll get better at it!

Straight talk helps connections progress. If you disclose that you've lost your job or been recently diagnosed with an illness, the other person will likely feel more comfortable revealing something personal, too. You might even learn that you share a challenge or concern—a struggle that you can talk about more. Exchanging confidences without fear of judgment is how friendships deepen.

There's no doubt that the reason I became so popular on the radio is because my listeners knew they could be open with me. When I'd greet callers with "You're on the air," they knew they could tell me anything and I'd never laugh, snicker, or put them down. Openness is what made my fans and me feel so close.

But please don't take this to mean that small talk is bad. Bantering about your day is the gateway to more in-depth conversations. So when you're comfortable going a little deeper, do it.

Hang Out

Part of what relationships need to become deeper and more meaningful is quality time. What I mean by this is unstructured time, the freedom to sit and talk without anywhere else to go and with nothing else to do. This also means having conversations with no set agenda or goal.

Sheila Liming, author of *Hanging Out: The Radical Power of Killing Time,* has described hanging out this way: "Daring to do not much and daring to do it in the company of other people."

Daring? It *is* daring! And it's hard to believe that hanging out takes thought and work. But it does. I refined my ability to hang out in Parisian cafés. The French make a point of practicing the art of conversation over coffee. As students at the Sorbonne, we were so poor that we'd go to a café and two of us would sip one espresso. We'd sit there for hours commenting on the passersby and talking about writers, painters, ideas. It was an incredible time.

When I was older and in New York, one of my favorite places to spend time was Elaine's, a restaurant on Manhattan's Upper East Side that was often visited by celebrities. I had a friend, Josh, who had a reserved table, and I'd join him every so often. I'd lose track of time just talking and getting to know people. Some people I'd see again, and those people I got to know even better. You never knew who might stop by the table, and that was part of the fun. The conversations were fabulous and freewheeling.

But I think it's important to keep in mind what I never talk about. I don't like gossip. I don't like venting about errands and chores that have to get done—that's so boring! And you already know how much I dislike complaining.

Is there a restaurant or coffee shop near you where you could just hang out? Maybe start small. Invite one friend, and that friend invites a friend, and see how your table grows!

Grease the Wheels

Speaking of restaurants, restaurant owners can teach us a thing or two about creating enduring relationships. Whenever I went to Spago in Beverly Hills, one of Wolfgang Puck's fabulous restaurants, I would get a free smoked salmon hors d'oeuvre. It's not the only reason that I and so many other celebrities would go to Spago, but it helped. And later, after the meal was complete, Wolfgang always came over to my table. We'd speak in German for a little bit, and I loved it.

Should you try to buy your way into friendship? If need be, I say yes. Let me explain.

If several of your co-workers are going out after work, and normally everybody buys their own drinks, you'll score some points with the group by picking up the first round. Is it a bribe? I don't think so. I just think it will help you curry favor and be thought of more positively, like what Wolfgang Puck does so well at Spago. His overture was kind but calculated. It made me like him even more, so that I kept going back to his restaurant whenever I could.

A modified version of this approach can work for you, too. I'm not suggesting you spend so much money that you can't afford to pay the rent, but for the price of a few glasses of wine, you might ease the path to building new and worthwhile relationships.

Throw Parties

When your birthday is approaching, if nobody has offered to make plans, it might be tempting to spend the day by yourself and pout. But you have to take action. Tell everyone you know that your birthday is coming up. Throw yourself a party if necessary. If all else fails, go to a neighborhood bar and announce, "Today's my birthday. This round's on me!" I guarantee people will celebrate with you. And you know what else will happen? The next time you go back to that bar, people will remember and welcome you.

Of course, your birthday only comes around once a year, which leaves a lot of other party-planning possibilities. Invite people to celebrate even the silliest of holidays with you. In the month of May, there's Eat What You Want Day and Chocolate Chip Day. In June, there's Iced Tea Day, and my favorite, Onion Rings Day. (If you want to know why this is closest to my heart, just google "Dr. Ruth" and "onion rings"!)

People might think it a little strange to get together for such harebrained reasons, but then again, if the party sounds fun, they're likely to come. And since deepening your connections is the goal, I say it's smart to be a little creative with how you go about doing it.

Work at Compromise

If you spend a lot of time by yourself, you have something in common with big shots and celebrities: You often get what you want when you want it.

This similarity could be one of the reasons why you're lonely.

What's for dinner? It's up to you. Should you watch TV or read a book? You decide. And on and on. After a while, you become used to a life without friction. You may hardly have to compromise at all.

But compromise builds relationships. When two people don't share the same opinion, there's a period of negotiation that takes place. There's a give-and-take. If you don't have experience compromising, you might become pigheaded. You might become sullen or angry when you don't get your way. None of this is going to help you build and maintain connections.

Every relationship requires compromise if it's going to last. The next time you have a disagreement with a friend or family member, I want you to review it carefully. Were you being too aggressive? Were you looking only to have things your way? I am not saying you should constantly put your needs and wants last. Not at all. But I do want you to decide which battles are important and which ones to let slide. My goal for you is to become adept at the fine art of compromise so you're best positioned to build and enhance your relationships.

Stick with Honesty

When Fred and I were dating, I deceived him. I still consider myself lucky that my little plot didn't end our relationship. I had invited Fred to a homemade dinner. My goal was to impress him, but because I am a terrible cook, I conspired with a distant relative to prepare the meal and pass it off as my own handiwork. Forever afterward, as he was forced to eat all the awful meals I created, he'd bring up the incident when I hoodwinked him into believing that I had made him dinner from scratch.

I realize that this is not the biggest lie in the world, and perhaps you were hoping for something more scandalous, but my sneakiness upset Fred so much that he never stopped bringing it up. I wasn't yet a Westheimer, but it was the Westheimer Maneuver he never forgave. I never should have done it. I was stupid, and the risk was too large. He could have ended our relationship because I had undermined his trust. I got off easy, and I hope you learn from my mistake.

Even lying by omission is a problem. I've always been scrupulous about saying that while I'm entitled to put *Dr.* in front of my name, I'm not a medical doctor. My doctorate is in education. And while I am a seasoned therapist, I never wanted anyone to think that I was providing MD-type advice. If you make yourself out to be something you're not, you're going to be found out. And there's a decent chance that the discovery will end the relationship. It's just not worth it.

Solid connections are built on honesty and transparency. When you're beginning relationships, if you feel the need to pretend that you're richer or more important than you really are, then the people you're hoping to impress aren't the friends and lovers you ought to be with.

Every time you're together, your ego is going to suffer because you'll know that they'd think less of you if they knew the truth. So while I wouldn't tell you to paint the bleakest picture of yourself when meeting someone new, it's easy enough to skirt subjects or activities that will make you look less than fabulous.

Always tell the truth, but maybe not everything all at once. Reflecting on that evening with Fred, after we ate, I could have mentioned to him that I had gotten help with dinner and that he was worth the extra effort. That would have been the better choice. It might have avoided the next thirty-plus years of his near-constant ribbing if I had been honest a lot sooner!

Tell White Lies, Sometimes

In 1947, after living on one kibbutz (south of Tel Aviv) and spending another year on a different kibbutz (next to Haifa), I moved to Jerusalem. I was thrilled to be there but soon got very lonely. I felt like a speck. I remember walking around on Friday nights by myself and looking into the windows of all the houses lit with Shabbat candles. *They all have families. They all have somebody to be with. Why can't I?*

But some aspects of my Jerusalem experience were wonderful. It's where I enrolled in a seminary to become a kindergarten teacher and made many new friends. Yet as my adult life was beginning to take shape, the political situation was growing increasingly tense. On November 29, 1947, the United Nations adopted a plan that paved the way for the British to leave Palestine and divide the land into two states—Jewish and Arab. Because there was so much unrest in the wake of this massive change, Jewish civilians were encouraged to join the Haganah, the precursor to today's Israel Defense Forces (IDF), so that's what I did. (I know you're wondering what any of this has to do with telling white lies and loneliness. Be patient with me. The reason for this story is coming.)

After basic training, I was given many jobs, including messenger and sniper (I still remember how to break down a rifle). I was never injured until the following year, when Israel declared itself a state. Then, on June 4, 1948, my twentieth birthday, I was caught up in a bomb blast. Three people were killed, one of whom was standing right next to me. I felt an excruciating pain in both my legs. Blood covered my feet. The top of one foot had been blown off and pieces of shrapnel were stuck all over my body, including my neck. I underwent surgery and have always felt grateful that I didn't lose either foot. (OK, here comes the point of my story.)

My recuperation was long, and while I was getting better, I became infatuated with one of the nurses taking care of me—a strong man, handsome and blond. Maybe because I had been without my family since I was a little girl, perhaps because I felt so isolated living in Jerusalem as a young woman, I craved his affection and attention. In order to get him to spend as much time with me as possible, I pretended that I needed a little more help than I did. This was my white lie. I lied so I'd feel less lonely. After I was released from the hospital, the nurse and I became romantically involved, at least for a time.

To me, the white lie I told was acceptable. A few extra minutes with me wasn't keeping him from providing critical care to other patients. There were triage nurses for the most serious cases, I knew. How do you tell whether a lie is white, meaning unharmful? It's pretty simple. Consider the day the lie is discovered. Will people think less of you? Might they never want to see you again? Or will they grin and leave your relationship intact?

I am not suggesting that you go around spewing white lie after white lie to win over possible friends and lovers. But if someone suggests you go to the movies to see a romantic comedy, and you detest these kinds of films, saying you like them just demonstrates your ability to compromise. Like my white lie, yours is victimless, and it's unlikely to come back to bite you.

Forgo One-Night Stands

I have long campaigned against having sex on the first date. This is even more important advice if you're lonely.

Some people use the dating scene looking only for physical contact. Once they get what they want, they move on. Casual sex may feel very good in the moment, but afterward, you might feel even lonelier than before.

Sex is emotional. When you're intimate, it's common to envision a future with the other person. But if it turns out that sex was the only thing that brought your partner to the bedroom, you're going to feel worse because your hopes of a more significant relationship have been dashed. You're better off avoiding such situations in the first place and making it a point not to have sex too quickly.

And while love at first sight does exist, more often than not, people need time to assess each other. Someone could seem very nice at first but have a hidden and horrible temper. It's always better to wait and gather more information. Assuming the relationship builds, there'll be plenty of time to have great sex. Until then, I want you to take your time and protect your heart.

Continue Having Sex!

Sex is the glue of romantic relationships. It makes us feel close to our partner. And while some older couples who no longer have sex maintain good relationships, others don't. Without this glue, they become estranged. Each person, no matter how attached and in love they once were, becomes progressively lonelier.

Feelings of disconnection caused by a lack of intimacy are avoidable. For a time, I was actively involved in a clinic at Bellevue Hospital in the Department of Geriatrics to help older adults improve their sex lives. Some men had difficulty obtaining and maintaining an erection (though Viagra came along and certainly helped that group), and quite a few women needed help managing painful vaginal dryness. But with our expert support and information, they could still have sex. Increasing the amount of touching helps. Introducing sex toys such as vibrators and masturbators is useful. And by including the application of a lubricant as part of sex play, couples are able to rediscover great sexual pleasure. What I learned at Bellevue is that you *can* teach older people new tricks, and these new tricks have the ability to reignite passion and rebuild connection.

As you age, it's essential to appreciate the warmth and closeness that having sex brings, even if the intensity of the experience—and the experience itself—is different from when you were younger. Try to make adjustments. See how it goes. If you're still having problems, seek out professional help so that you can stay sexually active as long as possible. Not only will it feel good, but it will also go a long way toward keeping your relationship vibrant and healthy, and you and your partner from feeling needlessly lonely.

Keep the Old

As you've come to know, I am still in touch with Putz, my first boyfriend. He and I met at that children's home in Switzerland, and we became a couple, as much as two kids in an orphanage with very strict rules could become a couple, when I was about twelve.

Having Putz take a liking to me was a wonderful surprise. I had always thought I was too ugly-looking for any boy to want anything to do with me. But he was attracted to me and I was very attracted to him. I remember all the kids were involved in a sewing project one day, and I intentionally placed the piece of fabric I was working on over my upper thighs and lap—not on the table in front of us—so Putz could sneak a quick feel without anyone seeing.

The two of us didn't remain a couple the whole time we were in the orphanage. (I had a tendency to be a little bossy and he soon found someone else.) But we've remained friends all of these years. Even though he settled in Haifa and I made a life for myself in New York, every time I traveled to Israel, which was yearly, we carved out time for a visit. He's one of very few people left on earth who knows what my life was like when I was a child. We have a shared history, which is so important for combating loneliness.

If you can, I urge you to keep old lovers and friends close. I know this is not possible or advisable for everyone. There are very good reasons for cutting people off completely. I am encouraging you to consider the value of keeping old relationships if they were good ones. If the only reason you've severed ties is the passage of time or distance, I'm pushing you to reconsider your decision and get back in touch.

Why should you keep friends and exes in your social sphere? To me, they're like money in a rainy-day savings account. You never know when you're going to find yourself in need of a dear old friend who knew you and cared for you way back when. Yes, make new friends, but keep the old. They become living, breathing pieces of scaffolding that keep you from crumbling when you're feeling especially alone.

Make Yourself More Friendly

What kind of friend or romantic partner are you? Let's assume you're a great listener and you're funny and comfortable sharing your feelings. These are all great qualities. But if you're not generous with your time, none of the other stuff matters.

What happened to Pierre after he lost his wife illustrates my point. Before his wife passed away, he'd turn down many invitations. He was happily married and wasn't looking for additional activities or companionship. But after Joanne died, Pierre came to understand that he no longer had this luxury. He recognized he had to be the kind of person who accepts invitations. Some evenings he might have preferred to stay home with a good book, but more often than not, he was quite pleased that he pushed himself to go out. Being busy helped Pierre feel less lonely.

When I was a young single mother, I could have used my baby daughter as an excuse to stay home. But I decided I wouldn't do that. I chose to say yes to parties and just take Miriam with me, putting her to sleep in any spare bedroom. (It was a different parenting time!) I knew that cutting myself off from people I enjoyed would not be good for either of us. If I had stuck to myself all the time, I would have been doing nothing to alter my sense of isolation, that feeling that falls upon so many single parents.

If you're lonely, you may have to force yourself to be more friendly—to be more social. Nobody will come to your door on a white horse and whisk you away. You've been invited. The going is up to you.

Cast a Wider Net

When my radio show went from being taped to being live, I needed a producer to field listener phone calls. I was assigned a young woman, Susan Brown. Right from the start, Susan and I had to completely trust each other. We'd both be successful if we each did our job well. Not only did we make a great team, but we also liked each other a lot. We chose to have regular lunches together, usually in the NBC cafeteria, and we got even closer. The fact that I was a college professor and Susan had just graduated from college didn't stop us from becoming fast friends. I went to her wedding, and she and I are still friendly today. "You made me feel like an adopted daughter," Susan told me recently. "I wanted your motherly advice on getting married, on my career, and you were always willing to share it."

You must expand your thinking when it comes to the way friendships typically form. From the time we start school, our social circles are most often determined by age—students who are in the same grade as us or perhaps, as we get older, the parents of our child's friends. But why let yourself be put into a friendship box like that?

What's essential for forming new relationships is curiosity. *Don't judge a book by its cover.* Be on the lookout for cross-generational opportunities. They invite the sharing of experiences, wisdom, and perspectives. You don't have to work in radio to cultivate such friendships. You can find them right in your community.

Community

Y OU'RE LIKELY ALREADY PART OF SEVERAL COMMU-
nities that will be very helpful in your battle
against loneliness. In this section, I'm going to
teach you how to take off your blinders. I want you to
see the big picture—that meaningful connections are
waiting for you in places you've underutilized or completely overlooked.

All around you there are groups of people who come
together for specific reasons and purposes. There are
work communities (colleagues and professional net-
works); school communities (alumni associations and
student clubs); religious and spiritual communities
(churches, mosques, temples, synagogues, and other religious organizations); hobby communities (dancing,
cooking, gaming, running); support communities (grief,
addiction, caregiving, and other challenges); neighbor-

hood communities (senior centers, libraries, gardening clubs, and civic associations); and, of course, volunteer communities (soup kitchens, food pantries, blood banks, and animal shelters). Have you dabbled with any such groups? Is your participation spotty? *If your goal is to feel a sense of belonging, then you must take steps to belong.*

I appreciate that for many people being active in the community means volunteering to help those in need. But I'm giving you permission to simultaneously focus on *your needs*. When deciding what organizations or activities to join, make sure you consider how they'll help you build relationships. Your goal isn't to connect with as many people as possible. Your job is to investigate and filter. I want you to approach connection making like a treasure hunt. Look for the gems!

Over the years, people who came to me for therapy told me they often felt loneliest at home. Eating dinner in front of the television. Getting under the covers alone, night after night. My advice was always the same—leave.

Go out to dinner. Take a walk. Get outside. Go to the library. Go to the park. Beyond your front door is where all the people are.

Make Your Town Smaller

When I was young, I spent a lot of time living communally, first in the orphanage and later on one kibbutz, then another. It was impossible for anyone to go unnoticed. New York City was a completely different experience for me. I had to work exceptionally hard to introduce myself to neighbors and make meaningful connections. To do both, I made a critical discovery: I had to make New York City *feel* smaller.

I joined organizations. I participated in neighborhood groups. I became a board member of the YM&YWHA of Washington Heights and served as board president for eleven years. During this entire time (now fifty-five years and counting!), I've attended countless meetings and social gatherings and made many good friends as a result. Being part of the Y makes me feel more connected to New York City, like I truly belong here.

Your first order of business is to develop a smaller community within whatever larger communities are easiest for you to access. Have you ever gone to a neighborhood block party? If next week you didn't leave your living room, would anyone wonder where you are? If your answer to either question is "no," you must change your absentee status right now. You must *make your town smaller*.

Be Authentically You

I understand that getting involved in neighborhood organizations may feel like an impossibly large step. If you claim you're too busy, be sure to read the section that starts at the end of page 87. But if what's keeping you away is anxiety, that's a headwind of another sort. The best way to overcome this type of uneasiness is to choose a just-right volunteer opportunity. Don't pick a community activity only because you think it will look good on your résumé or be meaningful to someone else. Pick something that piques your interest. Your enthusiasm for the activity will drown out your nerves.

Sure, I understand that walking into a group of strangers can be terrifying. But consider this: The upside of volunteering is that the people you meet are usually kindhearted and welcoming. Individuals who are grouchy, snooty, or selfish generally have zero interest in giving back.

Be a Mentor

One of the proudest moments of my life was receiving my doctorate in education from Columbia University Teachers College. It's very clear to me why I did well in school. I worked hard, of course, but the other reason was that I was learning a subject I loved, and my degree was the ticket to getting what I most wanted—my first nonkindergarten teaching job.

I landed at Lehman College in the Bronx and quickly learned that being a teacher is one of the best jobs for being socially active and engaged in the community. Bright young people are energetic and will constantly challenge you to think and talk. It's impossible to be around students and not begin to share their joie de vivre, their zest for life. The great news is that you don't have to be a teacher to reap these benefits. You can be a mentor.

Mentoring programs welcome people just because they have valuable experiences to share. If you're an accountant (assuming you're great with numbers!), you can help children with their academics, specifically in math. Maybe you work in human resources and you can prep teens for job interviews and sharpen their cover letters. Or perhaps you could just give your time and listen. Be the person who shows up and really cares.

Like teaching, mentoring is rewarding because you know you're making a difference. You'll feel better about yourself. And mentoring is valuable, too, because it pushes you into new environments. When you're lonely, you don't just need company; you need intellectual stimulation. I've always craved this kind of excitement! In fact, I loved teaching so much that I never wanted to be a full-time sex therapist. I never would have had enough time to teach!

Commit to *Meaningful* Busyness

Too many people boast about being tugged in multiple directions all the time. But there are several reasons why running around frantically is a bad idea. For one, if your attention is diluted, your efforts may not add up to making much of an impact in your community. Second, you'll miss the hidden upside of all of your labor: using your sustained commitment to build richer and more substantive connections.

What does this look like in practice? It's pretty simple, really: If you volunteer every Tuesday night, for example, you will likely run into the same people again and again. A steady and consistent routine can help you build relationships that matter.

In addition to the Y, I've been a member of the committee to protect and manage Fort Tryon Park in northern Manhattan for twenty-five years. Fort Tryon Park is near my apartment, it's where I pushed Miriam and Joel around in a stroller, and it's where I continue to spend many afternoons soaking up the fresh air and sun. The park is important to me, and because of that, volunteering for it feels good. After my husband Fred passed away, the committee named a bench at the park in his honor. I enjoy going there to sit and meditate. If I hadn't volunteered for so many years, if I hadn't invested so much effort into these specific relationships, there's no way that bench would be there today.

Resist the temptation to flutter about town—dropping cookies off here, helping with a tag sale there. Be thoughtful with your time. Try to pick one organization to devote yourself to on a regular basis. Meaningful busyness will always matter more than just being busy.

Help Your Neighbors

The simple act of helping a neighbor can be a powerful antidote to loneliness and isolation. Start by becoming more observant. I don't want you to become a Peeping Tom, but I encourage you to look for ways to be helpful to the people who live closest to you.

If you have neighbors with a new baby, the next time you go to the store, ask if they need food, cleaning supplies, or diapers. Elderly neighbors might need assistance mowing their lawn or shoveling snow off their driveway. I have joyful memories of my mother kneading dough in our kitchen and then sending me off to the neighborhood bakery because we didn't have an oven in our apartment. What a help that baker was to my family! I'm sure you can think of a million ways to be useful. What you do is not as important as offering to do something.

By lending a hand, you'll make new friends. Plus, doing good deeds will definitely lift your spirits. Loneliness can worm a hole in your heart and undermine your self-confidence. It might feel as if you don't make a difference to anyone. If you devote even a little bit of time to helping your neighbors, you'll begin to feel better about yourself and restore your sense of value.

Feign Needs

Just as my family benefited from the generosity of that neighborly baker, I want you to be open to receiving help, too—even if you have to invent a reason to ask for assistance.

If you're too self-reliant, if you're too proud, you're losing opportunities to meet people in your community and possibly forge new relationships. Sure, you can order a container of milk and get it delivered, but how about asking the person next door for a quarter of a cup of milk to finish that cake you're baking? And then you can even drop off a slice as a thank-you.

A word of caution, however: If you're like me and don't really enjoy mixing, stirring, or sautéing (not even when Miriam and Joel were small did I spend any more time in the kitchen than I had to), you might find it more authentic to borrow a hammer or screwdriver. You get the idea!

Those moments when you pick up that extra egg or air mattress are precious. They are pockets of time to deepen connections. And it doesn't matter what you ask for. Just make sure the favor you're requesting is easy to execute.

Reinvest in Faith

I mentioned at the beginning of this chapter that I deliberately joined organizations to make New York City feel smaller. If you haven't looked in a while, you might be surprised by the wide variety of nonreligious events taking place at houses of worship these days. Houses of worship are relationship magnets!

Many activities have little or nothing to do with reciting prayers. Mixers for young adults in their twenties and thirties. Field trips and vacations for learning and exploring. Movie nights and more. Houses of worship are gathering spots. They're social hubs. They're places where you can meet people who live nearby—maybe not in your exact neighborhood, but certainly in the general vicinity.

I do realize we are a society that's been steadily moving away from formal religion for a long time. This is also true of many Western European countries. I also recognize that there's no requirement that you join a house of worship in order to connect with people who share your religious beliefs. (I haven't been heavily involved in any one synagogue in a while, though for a time I did belong to three. If one rabbi asked why he hadn't seen me at Shabbat services, I could always say that I was at one of the other ones!) But because they're social centers, they're definitely worth checking out and potentially adding to your connections-building repertoire.

Read Socially

The great news about being an adult is that you can read as much as you like without being ridiculed for it. *Geek.*

Nerd. Dork. Smarty-pants. While relentless name-calling can be brutal for children who prefer books over people, adults who are passionate about reading can suffer, too—but for different reasons. Reading is usually a solitary activity. We do it at home, in bed or on the couch. But reading can be communal, too, and I want you to turn your love of literature into a means of enlarging and fortifying your social circle.

In your community, or hopefully not too far away, there's a public library. Now, it's true you're supposed to be quiet, but not everywhere, especially if it has social programs that you can sign up for. Yoga classes. Knitting circles. Photography tutorials. Depending on what courses you take, you're likely to encounter neighbors who share your interests.

Independent bookstores have also gotten serious about attracting new customers. Quite a few serve coffee and beer to encourage people to stay for a while—to *hang out.* Some are purpose-built for growing and nurturing communities—readers who love romance books, mysteries, or history, or who identify as Black or LGBTQ.

And there are some very creative folks who have discovered other ways to use books to encourage social connections. In New York City, there's a program called Reading Rhythms. The tagline says it all: "Not a book club. A reading party." The reading parties feature live music and happen in parks and in bars and on rooftops. Even in tattoo parlors! The way it works is that everyone brings a book and reads to themselves, and then blocks of time are set aside for strangers to chat with one another about the book they're reading, first in pairs, then in larger groups.

To me, books are amazing. They can keep you fascinated for hours and hours. But if you're not careful, they can become one of the reasons why you're lonely. They can also cause a massive decorating problem, as they did for me. I once had so many books in my apartment that they could no longer fit on my bookshelves. Instead of getting rid of them, I just piled the overflow in a corner and then covered the stack, which was taller than me, with a blanket. I started joking around and calling the mound my private ski slope. (Eventually interior designer Nate Berkus redesigned a few areas of my apartment for his TV show and the ski slope melted away.)

Sit at the Bar

Bars have traditionally been great places to meet people. But sitting *at* the bar may be your best choice for making connections.

Nobody is made to feel ashamed because they've sat down alone at the bar. Because people sit side by side, at equidistant intervals, it's actually hard to tell who's alone and who's not. Everyone looks the same. You can strike up conversations more easily. And not just with the people who are sitting to your left and right. In front of you, too. The bartender is almost always good for conversation! (If you live by yourself, this is all especially helpful. You may have limited opportunities to talk out loud, to hear your own voice, to chat with another person. At the bar, you can eat a meal and count on conversation.)

Consider how different the social experience is when you're seated by yourself at a restaurant.

When you walk into a restaurant without a reservation, there's no way to avoid the host's or maître d's inevitable question: "How many are in your party?" And then again, once you've been shown to your table, the waiter or waitress will inquire if you're expecting a friend to join you. Within a minute of your answer, the second place setting is whisked away. All of these seemingly innocuous interactions can feel humiliating. You can avoid all of this by heading to the bar.

Bars are also popular spots to go on first dates. While a glass of wine can be good for making those initial encounters a little less tense, I've always cautioned against drinking too much. Too much alcohol can turn any outing into a disaster. (I once put my name on bottles of low-alcohol wine to bring attention to my point. It was called Dr. Ruth's Vin d'Amour. I've never been a big drinker, but it tasted pretty awful. There are much better low-alcohol brands on the market today.)

Admittedly, you may not want to enter a bar because the temptation to drink is too strong. While a variety of nonalcoholic drinks are available, you know your circumstances best, and if going to a bar might be a problem for you, then you shouldn't go. But I think bars are worth exploring. They offer so much more than drinks and food. They offer social activities like dancing, darts, pool, and trivia nights. So if you're able to go to a bar, and you haven't in a while, I suggest giving it a try. You might develop one or two meaningful relationships if you do!

Live in Daily Community

If you feel you've tried everything in your community to build connections and yet still feel like an outsider, you may want to explore a rather bold and alternative living arrangement.

There are approximately six hundred so-called intentional communities in North America, home to more than ten thousand people. No longer derided as "hippie communes," these developments offer residents the opportunity to share expenses, cook meals together, and, of course, build relationships. Many are home to people in their late teens, twenties, and thirties (though many attract people who are much older) and are built with shared interests in mind—living a more sustainable lifestyle or coexisting with more economic equality.

Also created to prioritize connections are specially built neighborhoods such as Culdesac Tempe. The development near Phoenix, Arizona, doesn't allow residents to park private cars, so spaces that would typically be used for parking and garages are instead used for shared firepits, bike and walking paths, restaurants, boutique shops, and courtyards for sitting and talking—amenities that are intended to help residents meet and increase feelings of belonging.

Intentional communities remind me of the kibbutz I lived on when I was a teenager. While I recognize they're certainly not for everyone, they offer a rather different way of living that may be well worth exploring.

You can find collectives in nearly every part of the country and world. The Foundation for Intentional Community maintains a database users can search by location (state or country), type of housing (shared or individual), and organizing principle (faith or social impact). You may also want to explore the Cohousing Association of the United States and the Global Ecovillage Network.

Go to the Office!

I think it's fantastic that there are so many conversations today about where to work—whether at home, in the office, or some combination of both. But for people who are suffering from loneliness, there's no better option than spending time with colleagues in person. I know that it's easier to take care of aging parents or young children when you eliminate the need to commute, but you also eliminate the possibility of running into people in elevators or at the mini kitchen.

The office is where potential friends are. You can have a cup of coffee with a co-worker. You can eat an impromptu lunch together. Back when I was doing my cable TV show, I would tape a few shows during the afternoon and then do another live show in the evening. After the day was finally over at 11:00 P.M., I always had wine and cheese sent to the studio so everyone involved in the production could feel a sense of accomplishment and togetherness. It's nearly impossible to replicate this kind of camaraderie when most or all of your colleagues hardly ever come to the office.

Working in person, while surely less convenient, should be high on your priority list. In fact, I urge you to work only for companies that require workers to come into the office every day or for some portion of the week. None of this fully remote business. My point of view certainly won't win me points with everyone, but that's OK. It may be more convenient to work without leaving your couch, but making the effort to do it in person can really help your social well-being.

Create Remote Connections

Even though I believe that working in person is best for combating loneliness, please know that I am not saying you're facing a lifetime of despair if you work remotely. There are many ways you can strengthen connections with co-workers—even with individuals whom you have little chance of ever meeting in person.

Bestselling author and organizational psychologist Adam Grant writes about the "Five-Minute Favor" in his book *Give and Take*. He says you can deepen your connections by being proactively generous with your time— either introducing people who'd benefit from knowing each other or just sending a heartfelt thank-you email that isn't expected but is sure to be appreciated. The goal is making work relationships, even those that exist solely online, much more personal and satisfying.

While the Five-Minute Favor is effective, it's not Adam's number one recommendation. "My favorite option is to run a Reciprocity Ring—an exercise created by sociologists Wayne and Cheryl Baker," he told me. The way a Reciprocity Ring works, whether participants are in person or not, is that a group of people makes "asks" for something they need or want and the group considers their own "knowledge, resources, and connections to help fulfill the request."

When Adam runs Reciprocity Rings with students at the University of Pennsylvania, where he teaches, he sticks large pieces of blank paper all over the room and invites everyone to anonymously write down their personal or work-related requests. A few of his students were interviewed about the experience and said they enjoyed the exercise because it helped them get to know their classmates on a deeper level. Goals such as "New ways to manage chronic pain" or "Learn how to play the guitar" fueled conversations students might not have had otherwise.

Reciprocity Rings build connections because they make everyone who participates feel good—the "askers" and the "givers." Wayne Baker says the best number of participants to conduct a Reciprocity Ring via Zoom is unlimited, as long as you create breakout groups that are no larger than five to six people.

Cultivate Friends at Work

I've worked outside the home my entire life and met some of my dearest friends because I did. Planned Parenthood, where I was hired as a research associate in 1967, was my first exposure to talking with clients about contraception and abortion. Within one week of taking the position, I knew the job was perfect for me. I loved sex education and talking about family planning. I also enjoyed spending time with so many people! But another benefit of the role was getting to know my boss, Stuart Cattell, and taking our relationship far outside the walls of Planned Parenthood.

You may recall that my late husband Fred and I spent time together at Lake Oscawana, about sixty minutes north of our apartment in New York City. It turned out that Stuart lived close by, and he and I became friends outside of work as a result. The times that I was up at the lake, we hiked together, talked a lot, went sailing, and enjoyed plenty of great meals. Sometimes Fred would join us; other times he did his own thing.

Today I would never advise a subordinate and supervisor to spend time together as Stuart and I did, even if the relationship is platonic, as ours was. Times are different and I don't want anyone to get into trouble. That said, it remains a very good idea to be open-minded about making friends with your peers at work, since work is where you spend so much of your time.

If you work in a large corporate office, employees may be offered opportunities to join affinity groups—maybe ones focused on new parenthood or women's empowerment. Join one of these communities! You might hit it off with a colleague and decide to catch a baseball game one day after work or go to a concert. And remember what I mentioned on pages 66–67 about the importance of paying attention to context? Workplace friends have a better chance of becoming real-life friends when they spend time together outside their shared business environment. Watch out for these kinds of moments. They will help you build rewarding peer relationships.

If you work in an office that doesn't offer formal ways for co-workers to mingle, you'll have to create opportunities on your own. We didn't have formal social programs at Planned Parenthood, either, but we had something else that, looking back now, was a real advantage to feeling connected at work: the absence of computers. To get work done, we had to get up from our desks and talk with colleagues face-to-face.

Throughout your workday, you need to push yourself to stand up from your desk and walk down the hallway. Say hello to colleagues. Ask how their work is going. Offer to help with a difficult assignment. These are all painless actions, yet I promise they will make your work environment a less lonely place.

Cultivate Friends Outside Work

I recognize that making friends at work may not be right for you. If work is the reason you're feeling isolated, build a support network outside of it. Join professional organizations that are designed to bring together people who are at the same stage in their careers, work in the same field, or are grappling with similar issues.

Ann Shoket is the CEO of a community of women and nonbinary leaders called TheLi.st. Just as I suggest in "Be Vulnerable" with regard to relationships with family, Ann says the ability to be honest about career-related challenges helps women feel less lonely at work. She cautions, though, that many women find these types of conversations easier to have when they're with colleagues who don't work for the same company. "We're often in competition at work—vying for resources, attention, and roles that are scarce. These stakes make seeking outside perspectives tremendously valuable and an important way to build a feeling of real togetherness," Ann explains.

Work doesn't have to be a place that makes you miserable and lonely. By joining a professional group, even your local chamber of commerce, you'll create opportunities for sharing your highs and lows. I know being candid isn't easy. But when you allow yourself to be fully seen, you might just expand your number of connections—and deepen them, too.

Go to Conferences

You may work for a business that gives employees the chance to attend professional development conferences. I say, go. Go right now! Don't turn down this very good opportunity for meeting new people because you prefer your home to a hotel. That's an excuse, and excuses hold you back from achieving your goal—forming new and meaningful connections.

And by the way, conferences aren't just for work. There are gatherings for people who are passionate about genealogy, scrapbooking, comic books, gaming, and other pastimes.

I've been a lover of music my entire life, and because of that, I've attended the North American Jewish Choral Festival many times. While the focus every summer is on singing, the festival acts as a typical conference in many ways: Participants hear the latest news from leaders in the field (nearly two dozen accomplished choirs attend from all over the world!), and there are always opportunities to turn strangers into friends.

My friendship with Matthew Lazar, the creator of the festival, became richer over the years because I've gone to these events—so much so that our friendship blossomed well beyond singing. We've shared many meals together and visited Tanglewood, the popular music space in western Massachusetts, numerous times. In 2015, he invited me to conduct a concert at Avery Fisher Hall at Lincoln Center by a group of four hundred student singers. The music made me cry. It reminded me so much of my father, transporting me back to my childhood in Frankfurt. I could almost feel my father holding my hand again as we walked to synagogue on Friday nights. Matty, as we all affectionately call him, made that memorable evening happen for me.

Making friends in a highly curated environment eases the path to friendship. Take advantage of this openness. Use each day to cultivate new connections. You already know you have interests in common, so you've already got plenty to talk about!

Repurpose Community Networks

The reason why Nate Berkus decided I was a good candidate for his TV show is because I'm something of a pack rat. When he came to my apartment in 2011, I was so self-conscious about how overstuffed it was with papers, binders, and tchotchkes that I rarely invited friends over anymore. The clutter was cutting me off from my social life. But Nate put me at ease when he said I didn't have to get rid of everything. He taught me that I just needed to find new ways to manage my cherished belongings. This lesson has a surprising application to this conversation we're having about loneliness.

There's a good chance that you still have access to a few email lists and text chains that were once quite active but are no longer being used. Maybe somebody had a long stay in the hospital and you were in charge of updating friends and relatives about their condition. Or your child was on a soccer team and you had a contact list of parents to arrange carpools. These lists are excellent resources that can easily be put to innovative and deliberate use.

The people on these lists were probably not close friends. You may have enjoyed their company at the time but likely drifted apart because that reason for coming together ran its course. But as I've said, *keep the old*. Friendships are assets to be treasured. Instead of letting these lists go unused, send a brief update that would matter to members of the group. (For example, those soccer parents might love to hear about the new competitive travel team you discovered.) The replies will perk you up, and you might even get an invitation to grab lunch sometime. Deeper friendships will hopefully follow.

If you feel silly reaching out, keep in mind that we're all in this loneliness epidemic together. It's likely that at least one person on those lists is also longing for companionship. To that individual, your out-of-the-blue text or email won't be unwelcome at all; it will be much appreciated.

Join a Support Group

Sometimes, no matter how much of my guidance you follow, the people in your community might not be able to provide the kinds of connections you crave most. You might ultimately need to expand your definition of community to include support groups. There was a time when I needed the help of a psychiatrist, and I sought out a very good one. There's no shame in needing to alleviate a mental health issue any more than in needing to treat the flu.

Unlike the one-on-one therapy I received, support groups offer a concrete sense of belonging to a group. Everyone who signs up is willing to talk and listen and share—a perfect environment to work through individual challenges *and* possibly build connections. If you've gone through a crisis of some sort, like the death of a loved one, it can be beneficial to hear how others are navigating a similar experience. But I do have a big word of warning before you sign up.

A sex therapist like me is considered a behavioral therapist. I went through years of training to do my job. Running a support group well also takes a great deal of study, if you're going to do it with gravitas and expertise. A gathering of people who are permitted to spend an entire session griping about how awful their circumstances are—without being given the necessary tools for making their circumstances better—is not going to be helpful. Worse, it can be damaging.

I know this is controversial. I recognize the value of peer support. But peer support becomes worrisome to me when it's offered in the absence of trained facilitators, especially when participants are given bad advice and group leaders don't have the knowledge to correct it.

So what to do? If you're ready to join a support group, do so, but please make sure it's led by a professional who can move the conversation in a positive direction. When you find that trusted group, it might be the best community you'll ever find.

Technology

Y OU MIGHT ASSUME MY ADVICE IN THIS PORTION
would simply be to get rid of your technology.
But that's not the case. I don't view technology
as the enemy. Let me say right away, in case you're thinking that because I'm an older woman I feel otherwise, I
would never advise anyone to entirely stop using their
phone and laptop. These are necessary tools in today's
world. In fact, if you abstain completely, you may find
yourself the odd person out, and that won't help you
make connections, either.

I have more than 100,000 followers on X, so I can't
get on my high horse and condemn social media. It allows me to reach people in a way I could not otherwise.
But am I *friends* with them? If I were especially lonely,
would these individuals, most of whom I'll probably

never meet, help me overcome my sense of isolation? I think you know the answers.

Still, I do think there are ways technology can increase our connections to others, especially in-person connections, which will always be the most important. But what if you don't use much technology, or you use none at all? If you're a technophobe, I suggest you determine if a lack of technology is holding you back. There is an entire universe of invisible social activity happening all around you—invitations to food festivals, cultural events, and more—and if you're not joining in, you will be left out. Perhaps you already are.

Experts seem to agree that technology has become a major factor in causing loneliness. I don't disagree. But it's also true that it can add fuel to your social circle. If used with purpose, technology can enhance relationships. It all depends on whether you use these virtual interactions to build deeper in-person connections.

Break into Conversation Clusters

Outgoing people tend to have an easier time building social connections. Being reserved often makes it harder. But even if you're timid, there are always work-arounds. Perhaps I understand more than most the need to improvise. I'm very short and can't reach most of the shelves in my kitchen. But do I give up when I need something? Never. I use a stepladder. So what am I suggesting you do if you're shy? You need a party-ready version of my stepladder, one that is portable and will help you break into conversation clusters. *It CAN be done.*

Your phone is your stepladder. When you're at a party and feeling hesitant to approach a group of people talking, take out your cellphone and sidle up with a plan: Ask them to pose for a photo and tell them that you're taking it for the host. Nobody will refuse. After they're done posing and laughing, a window will open for you to introduce yourself. Voilà! You're suddenly part of the group!

Just knowing you have a "stepladder" in your pocket will make you feel bolder and more courageous. Even if you don't end up using it, your phone will give you a sense of fearlessness—that you're wearing an invisible superhero cape and have the ability to enter any conversation. It's your secret conversation-starting weapon.

Gift Yourself Seven Minutes

There's another way to boost your connections-making power at social gatherings—and this one requires that you leave your phone in your pocket, at least for a little while: Take seven minutes to become fully invested in a conversation before ending it.

The concept is that you must spend seven minutes talking with someone to determine if the conversation is worth continuing and before giving yourself an out by looking at your phone. The advice is not mine, but I pass it along here because the guidance is from one of the country's preeminent experts in digital technology and has the potential to change your life.

In the field of social science, computers, and cellphones, the best of the best is Sherry Turkle, founding director of the MIT Initiative on Technology and Self and author of numerous books, including *Alone Together: Why We Expect More from Technology and Less from Each Other,* a primer on how technology has created a new form of loneliness, and *Reclaiming Conversation: The Power of Talk in a Digital Age.* Sherry is a clinical psychologist, and her book *Reclaiming Conversation* is markedly helpful in so many ways. But the part that strikes me as the most important for the purpose of combating loneliness is her discussion of the so-called seven-minute rule, a strategy for sticking with a conversation that was told to her by a college student she interviewed for that book.

The student said that for her, seven minutes can feel excruciating. I understand what she means. There's no doubt it might seem like an eternity, especially if you believe there's nothing you and the other person have in common. But the lesson is to stick it out. After a mere 420 seconds, you might discover you went to the same camp or have mutual friends—promising kernels for any new relationship. The student admitted that when she has her cellphone with her, she can't abide by her own rule. This reinforced Sherry's concern that phones distract from our quest to build a less lonely life. "Conversation is the most human and humanizing thing we do," Sherry explained to me. As you likely know by now, I also believe this to be true.

Take Notes on Your Phone

Despite its drawbacks, your phone is the perfect device for keeping track of what's important to other people.

Take notes on your phone whenever friends and relatives mention a brand of clothing they like, a singer or band they love, or a restaurant they're dying to try. Instead of being stumped about what to get them for their birthday or the holidays (and turning to an impersonal present like a gift card), you'll be able to consult your list and buy or make something that shows how much you care and how intently you listen.

Gift giving is an opportunity to convey thankfulness and love. By carefully selecting a present, you're demonstrating that the recipient's interests are important to you, and because thoughtfulness builds closeness, your bond will grow stronger. But don't take notes while you're together. Stay in the moment and focus on your conversation. You can jot them down later, once you're home.

Talk More, Text Less

I've recommended strategies for using cellphones to both establish and deepen connections. But if you've paid close attention, you'll notice something quite ironic. So far, my recommendations haven't involved using your cellphone as an actual phone—*to call people*. Many of us prefer to text these days, but I strongly defend using your phone for its old-fashioned purpose. Hearing someone's voice has the power to make you feel less lonely.

The missing ingredient with texts is voice intonation. Words on a screen can communicate only so much. By using an enthusiastic or unenthusiastic tone of voice, you're able to give a completely different meaning to a word such as *yes*. A simple sigh before saying yes tells the other party that you really might not want to agree but feel compelled to. We learn as infants via mimicry that we can make our voices sound happy or sad, angry or tired. Humans have used pitch and tone to express feelings and communicate emotions since prehistoric times. To throw these vocal cues away in the twenty-first century makes no sense at all.

If you're on a crowded bus, I admit that texting is going to be preferable. But if you always text, your relationships will suffer. And while I am very well aware that you can use your phone to leave voice messages, I don't think audio recordings are replacements for phone calls. Sure, a voice memo is better than a text, but to someone as impatient as I am, waiting to receive a return voice message takes far too long.

By the way, there's a side benefit to talking on your phone. You might not think of it as a means to get your ten thousand steps in, but if you use the Dr. Ruth method, trust me, your step count will climb quickly. When I'm on the phone, I move back and forth incessantly. For me, talking on the phone has always been a form of exercise!

Use Emojis

When calling someone isn't possible or even desirable, using emojis in your texts is the next best thing for getting your point across and not being misunderstood. Emojis improve the quality of texts, approaching the positive nature of phone calls—allowing your messages to be conveyed as you intend. And when you communicate better, your relationships stand a better chance of growing even stronger!

The best way for me to explain this concept is to give you an example. If you text a one-word response to a question without including an emoji, you may come off as terse or dismissive. But if you text the same one-word response—but this time with an excited-face emoji—you are more likely to come off as eager and enthusiastic, which will feel very good to the person who is receiving your text.

What all of this comes down to is the importance of nonverbal cues in protecting and enhancing connections. Even the best actors in Hollywood use facial expressions to ensure audiences know exactly what their character is feeling, in addition to reciting their lines. (In this way,

emojis are also an effective replacement for eye contact.)
There are thousands of emojis—use some of them!

Remain Cool

Let's assume there's someone new in your life. If this
new friend or lover has also been lonely for a while, perhaps you can become very close in a short amount of
time. But it's more likely that this new connection has
friends and family, so he or she is not going to be able to
devote the time to completely fill in your social calendar.
If you come on too strong, always texting, this person
might decide that you're too needy and begin avoiding
you instead of spending time with you.

What I suggest you do at the beginning stages of any
relationship is show restraint. Don't text too often, and
when you do, make your texts very short. I know the
inclination is to reach out. It's a way we try to reassure
ourselves that we haven't been forgotten. But pay very
careful attention to the replies you get. How quickly do
they come? Do they demonstrate enthusiasm or apathy?
Unless this new person always writes back fairly quickly
and seems appreciative of your communications, you
are best served by backing off and remaining cool.

If you're very lonely, I understand that finding a
friend is like discovering a life preserver; you want to
cling to it for dear life. But even though your reaction is
understandable, you need to be patient. If you're not,

you might soon find yourself without this connection altogether. So no matter what, in the early stages of a relationship, try to relax and limit how frequently you text.

Immerse Yourself in Podcasts

Podcasts are a fantastic means to be entertained and informed, but some offer much more than music, commentary, and interviews. Some hosts build online communities and create experiences to foster connections between listeners. I want you to search for one or two podcasts on subjects that you care most about, and then do a little homework to determine if opportunities exist for fans to discuss episodes on Facebook or gather in person. Once you find them, don't be passive. Participate in conversations and go to events when they're offered.

Podcasting is an incredible innovation. If I were starting my radio program now, it most definitely would be a podcast! They invite discussion of pretty much any topic and make anyone listening feel less alone in their struggles. I do, however, warn about the temptation to listen to podcasts every time you're in a taxi or running errands. To build more connections, you must unplug your ears, at least sometimes.

Imagine this: You're on the checkout line at the grocery store. It's a very long line. The person standing next to you might want to start a conversation, hoping to commiserate, but they see AirPods in your ears. You may not be saying a word, but you're actually communicating plenty. You might as well be saying, *I'm not interested in speaking with you.* So you know what happens? Nothing. An opportunity foiled by technology. And that's my point.

You no doubt know that couples have met waiting for lattes at Starbucks. But for that to happen, your ears have to be available for conversation. So please, don't use your earbuds as a crutch. When you're trying to make new friends or meet a potential romantic partner, it might be best to listen to podcasts at home.

Chat with Your Seatmate

I love picking up new friends on airplanes! I've met all sorts of fabulous people just because we were assigned seats next to each other. On one flight, I met a dress designer who ended up making me two beautiful outfits. On another, I met a woman who was studying for a master's degree in social work. It turned out that she was Mormon, and I asked her to appear on my show so I could interview her about family life in the Mormon community. The next time you're on a long flight, I challenge you to chat with your seatmate. I'm not suggesting that you strike up a conversation about politics or ask anything too personal, but a little schmoozing couldn't hurt.

Banter of any kind might feel forced to you. I understand. But when the time feels right, push yourself to ask an open-ended question that invites chitchat. You might ask if she's heading home or away for work. If she says away for work, then you might ask about the type of work she does. You may discover you have shared professional interests. I was introduced to John Silberman, who became my lawyer and business adviser for a time, because of a recommendation I received on a plane. John and I have now been in each other's lives for more than forty years!

I recognize that breaking the invisible wall between strangers is harder than it used to be. We no longer have to rely on one another when we travel. Updated gate information is texted to our phones, and we can watch endless TV shows and movies to pass the time. (We were once forced to talk to one another when we were bored!) But here's what I say: When you make the decision to turn off your screen, you're better positioning yourself to make new connections.

I've never been a proponent of abstinence when it comes to sex, and I'm not arguing for abstinence when it comes to phones, either. So I am not saying you should turn off your phone when you're traveling. Your job is to find a middle ground between being entertained and being engaged with people around you. Maybe watch one TV show instead of the whole series. Even in friendship, someone has to make the first move. It might as well be you!

Be *Ruthlessly* Selective

Friends take effort, but you don't need to buy them. Yes, you can certainly spend money on birthday gifts and holiday presents (that's very generous of you and certainly helps grease the wheels), but allowing your bank account to become depleted is never a sign of a healthy relationship, one that is built on mutual affection and respect.

I've heard many stories of lonely people being taken advantage of when they get sucked into digital gaming. In some contests, players compete in front of live audiences and vie for virtual gifts. These virtual gifts cost real money, and if you spend enough, you'll likely be showered with praise. I know this attention feels good— you are being seen and it feels like you're being valued— but it's not real. It's meant to keep you glued to the screen, spending more and more money.

But Dr. Ruth, I hear you say, *I've made so many friends this way. If I cut them out of my life, I'll have no friends at all.*

If you were someone who wasn't suffering from loneliness, you might have a point. But you are suffering. And investing so much time with these types of friends isn't what you need. You need to retreat from these activities and find the interest and energy to meet people face-to-face. You must be ruthlessly selective.

Research Interest-Specific Groups

Now that you've decided to be choosier about how to spend your time and with whom, I encourage you to use websites and apps that are purpose-built for creating connections around specific passions and goals.

One that is very popular is Meetup. Meetups can center around nearly any interest or activity, from drinking coffee to practicing a foreign language to going for a walk. You can find pickup basketball games or running partners. Meetups are especially helpful when you move to or visit a new town or city. An instant way to connect with people—people you might really like and who live nearby!

What I find terrific about these platforms (Meetup is not the only one) is that most of the people who organize activities take their roles very seriously. They try hard to make everyone who shows up feel comfortable. They'll greet you and introduce you to others, and within seconds of arriving, you're part of a group.

Meetups are full of people who are open to making new friends. Will anyone else be lonely, seeking to establish a long-term, meaningful relationship? Some might be. Some may not. But I can tell you this: The odds are in your favor that at the very least you'll establish a few new relationships and have a good time.

Use Dating Apps

Dating in your later years (or any time of life, for that matter) can be daunting. After my husband Fred died, I eventually tried to meet someone new. I went on Jdate, the online dating app for Jewish singles. At the time I used it, it was just a website. It's gotten much bigger since then!

While a few profiles interested me (one man was a therapist, another was five foot two—a real plus, at least for me!), I didn't find a match that excited me enough to keep pursuing. I didn't force a relationship just because being with someone was better than being alone. I am—and you are—too good for that.

I realize that when you're older you may feel a sense of urgency to find a partner. You may not give yourself the opportunity to be choosy because time isn't on your side. My advice: Don't jump into a relationship just because your timeline is compressed. Adjust your time-table. Let go of the urge to land an OK mate when you should be patient and wait for someone who's right for you. Bad relationships can make you feel even more lonely than being alone.

And while my Jdate experience didn't go very far, don't let my experience discourage you. I have friends who've been very successful using dating apps (there are so many you can try), in particular friends who are in their sixties and seventies. The common thread among all of them is that they fully embraced their age and took their time.

Write Honest Profiles

The upside of dating when you're older is that you come to the dating scene much more clearheaded than when you were in your twenties. You know what you want because you have lived experience. This type of self-awareness allows you to be direct in how you present yourself online. If you are a young person reading this, let my personal experience and years working as a therapist save you considerable heartache.

I don't enjoy being in the kitchen, so pretending that I enjoy cooking won't help me find the right partner. I'm better off being honest about my love of skiing. Likewise, if you dislike the beach and you come across a profile of someone whose favorite vacation pastime is sunbathing on a chaise, don't even bother with a first date. You will save yourself a lot of time and energy. And while I realize that dating apps make it very easy to date and keep dating, I advise you to be very careful, and not just when it comes to contraception and sexually transmitted diseases.

Serial dating can make you feel lonely, even more lonely than if you didn't date at all. A constant cycle of new relationships prevents meaningful bonds from forming. It may also cause you to feel a sense of emptiness and a lack of self-worth. These are lessons for everyone, no matter if you're twenty-five or seventy-five. You'll increase the likelihood of finding your forever partner on dating apps if you're 100 percent honest about what you like and what you don't. No pretending!

Go Sightseeing

Book a trip with a tour group or go on a guided tour of your own city. In New York you could go on a historical walk of the Lower East Side, complete with pizza and bagels, or a Harlem walking tour with stops that highlight the Harlem Renaissance and the civil rights movement. You can also use apps, including Google Maps and Yelp, to design your own outing. If you're feeling lonely, invite a friend to come along—a great motivator for getting outside! "Sightseeing is one of the most popular ways to share an experience with someone," podcast host and author Gretchen Rubin reminds us in her wonderful book *Life in Five Senses*.

One last recommendation: On your next visit to New York, bring your family to my neighborhood, Washington Heights, for a trip to the Cloisters, a fascinating medieval art museum in Fort Tryon Park. And when you are there, be sure to rest awhile on the bench dedicated to Fred. It's very close by, an easy stroll from the Margaret Corbin Circle entrance. It would mean a lot to me that you visited.

Track Your Time

Yes, we must live with technology, but we must simultaneously be honest with ourselves about how much we're using it. I support keeping your digital life active, but always with purpose and never at the expense of in-person connections.

The simplest way to find out if you're spending too much time online is to monitor yourself and write down the results. I wish I could tell you there's a certain number of hours that researchers agree makes screen time all good and completely harmless. There isn't. And while no exact number exists, I'd be willing to bet that if you're on your phone so much that it's interfering with your ability to sustain friendships and romantic relationships, you'll see a pattern you'll want to improve when you look at your numbers.

To anyone who says that zero is the only number of hours to spend on technology every day, I completely and emphatically disagree. As I've shared, we can harness technology to build connections. But tracking your time is important because it's a form of accountability. Someone is looking over your shoulder. Someone has your best interests at heart. And that someone is you.

Your Monthly Calendar

HOLIDAYS PROVIDE TIMELY OPPORTUNITIES FOR connecting with others. Some days are obvious (the Fourth of July and Thanksgiving), but celebrations such as World Compliment Day and National Friendship Day are wonderfully relationship building, too. Certain holidays can also intensify loneliness (if your mom or dad has died, Mother's Day or Father's Day might feel especially isolating), and for those times, it's particularly helpful to plan ahead.

I've naturally begun with January. Perhaps you're making a New Year's resolution to build more connections. That's wonderful! But what if you're reading this book in June? Should you put off your search for companionship for another six months? Of course not. I'm an impatient person. I want you to jump to the month you're in right now and just get started.

But I also want you to understand that ridding yourself of loneliness isn't going to happen overnight. You must accept that it's going to take time and acknowledge that success will come only from keeping up the work. This is precisely why "Your Monthly Calendar" will be so helpful to you. No matter the month, no matter the season, there is an immediate and actionable opportunity for making connections. And if you happen to like a suggestion in a month that's far away, go for it. Don't waste a single minute.

Look at the next twelve months as a healthy dessert next to the Menu for Connection. Each offers a fresh chance to beat loneliness and live a happier and more meaningful life.

January

There is no better New Year's resolution than deepening your circle of connections. "Today you" must take care of "future you."

But don't feel bad when you stumble. You can begin now, begin again later, and then begin once again after that. When I make resolutions, I know that I am not going to follow them! There's no need to be perfect. *Be less judgmental* of yourself and stay committed to your goal even when you hit setbacks.

Sure, take advantage of this new start, but don't put all your hopes into it. Keep going when you let your best efforts slide. Continue making the kinds of choices that will benefit you throughout the year—and your life.

February

If the thought of Valentine's Day fills you with dread, do what I do: Call a friend who is also alone and plan to do something enjoyable together. Order in dinner. Watch a movie you both love. And if you eventually decide to go out to a restaurant or bar, who knows, you might even meet somebody!

All of this advice aside, it might help to know that I actually don't believe in Valentine's Day. I think it's a commercial invention that you shouldn't worry about. Restaurants charge more money for dinner and flower companies make all kinds of extra profit. And being bombarded with red and pink hearts all over the place can make people who are not in a relationship feel even more lonely.

Regardless, I understand this day might be hard for you, and because of that, let me offer two more opportunities for lightening your mood.

First, plan a party. My friend Judy Licht, a former television reporter and anchor, hosts a very fun women-only Valentine's Day party every year. You don't have to be single. You don't have to be widowed or divorced. The gathering is just a fun opportunity for friends to express their love to one another.

And last, consider babysitting for a single parent or

a couple with children. You'll not only feel good about yourself because you're lending a hand, but you'll also be so distracted you may even forget for a moment that you don't have a romantic partner—at least right now.

March

March 1 is World Compliment Day. Giving compliments is yet another secret weapon in combating loneliness, just like using your phone to take pictures at parties.

Telling people you like their shirt or mentioning that you like their haircut makes them feel good about themselves, and their positive mood will be aimed in your direction. (Studies show that we often underestimate how good compliments make others feel.) Just pick something you see—a hat, a sweater—and offer a few kind words about it. It's nonthreatening, it's simple, and it works. Plus, it's free!

But compliments don't have to be obvious. The one compliment I most like to receive is that my work as a therapist is taken seriously despite the fact that I am so short. Many times I feared that my work would be dismissed because of my size. If you see me, that's what I'd most like to hear.

April

April 22 is Earth Day. And while there is no shortage of community activities to grab your attention (trail cleanups, nature scavenger hunts), I'd like you to consider spending the day, or at least a portion of it, completely alone. This advice may sound absurd. *But Dr. Ruth, why are you telling me to spend even more time by myself? This is a book about combating loneliness!*

Yes, I know. And no, I haven't lost my mind. The truth of the matter is that virtually any kind of green open space can make you feel less lonely. This is because nature offers alternative ways to connect with the world around us. Being outside—hearing the wind rustling leaves, watching a stream tumbling over rocks—increases our overall sense of well-being. I've always loved being in nature. Focusing on the clouds and squirrels—all of it helps me forget my troubles, at least for a while.

If you're looking for a special spot to commune with the great outdoors, there's one garden in New York City that I like most of all. Friends of my daughter own a nursery in the Netherlands, and when they developed a new kind of tulip, they named it after me. (It is short and has vibrant colors!) Hundreds of these cheerful flowers were planted not too far from my apartment in my beloved Fort Tryon Park. They named the garden Dr. Ruth's Tulips. Maybe on Earth Day you can visit my tulips.

May

If you're grieving the loss of your mother, Mother's Day can make you feel especially lonely. My mother's name was Irma Hanauer, and I remember what she said to me when she put me on that train in Germany to save me from the Nazis: "Be good. Study hard. It will be nice in Switzerland. And we will see each other again."

Her words gave me hope and sustained me through many dark times. Looking back now as I approach my hundredth birthday, what I mostly feel is awe. Her courage astounds me. I can't imagine feeling so afraid for my daughter's life that the best option was putting her on a train to a place I'd never been, to a land and people I didn't know.

When I remember my mother, though, I don't dwell on any of this. I focus on the wonderful ten years we had together. Given my experiences with loss (both personally and working with so many clients over the years), I have three pieces of advice if you're feeling lonely on Mother's Day.

First, be grateful. If you had a positive relationship with your mother, rejoice in that knowledge. (Many clients I treated in private practice did not have good relationships with their mothers, so this shouldn't be taken for granted.)

Second, set aside time to think about your mother, even if there's been a rift in your relationship or you've never been emotionally close. Loneliness burrows deeper when you ignore your emotions and pretend you're OK when you're not.

And finally, if you don't begin to feel better and a

little more connected to your mother, pick up the phone and call a friend. But don't reach out to someone who will cut you off after a few minutes because they're too busy. Choose a person who will let you talk and talk. I predict you will gradually feel less alone if you take my advice.

June

For many people, food increases sensations of connection and love. If you're missing your dad on Father's Day, no matter the reason—maybe you're estranged or he's passed away—you can use your senses of taste and smell to feel closer to him, and in doing so, I hope you will feel a little less lonely.

My father, Julius Siegel, often made me a special meal when I was growing up. Concerned about my growth, he prepared runny soft-boiled eggs and cut bread into long strips for dipping. It was meant to spur my appetite, which was often nonexistent when I was young. (Now I eat plenty. Especially chocolate!) When I think back, I also remember my father buying me vanilla ice cream every Friday night on the way to synagogue before the sun went down.

Are there dishes or desserts that remind you of your father? By eating these foods, by savoring them, you might begin to rebuild your connection and feel it even more strongly.

July

During my journey to America on the French ship *Liberté*, I was in fourth class, and those of us housed way down below weren't allowed up on the top deck. But the night we were due to arrive in New York Harbor, Dan (the man who became my second husband) and I sneaked up top and waited all night, hidden in the dark, to catch sight of the Statue of Liberty. There was no way I was going to miss the view the next morning. I was overjoyed to be coming to the United States and was so thankful to the U.S. Army for defeating the Nazis. I wanted so badly to see the country where these brave GIs had come from to rescue us!

People in the United States often forget how lucky they are to live in a free society. You may be lonely, but it's within your power to change your circumstances. You don't have to be afraid that your neighbors might tell the secret police if you associate with the "wrong sort" of people or that your co-workers will report you for mingling with the wrong crowd. For the most part, while outside forces certainly contribute to feelings of loneliness, we all have the freedom to make positive changes in our lives, to make ourselves happier. This autonomy is one reason I like to celebrate Independence Day. The holiday is also a great excuse to nurture connections in your community!

Join a Fourth of July committee. Plan the local parade or help keep the fireworks display safe. Since organizing these types of events usually takes a while, you'll be planning with the same group of people, and that consistency will strengthen your ties to neighbors. On a smaller scale, if you know that the mom or dad next door is serving in the military, you might include his or her spouse and children in your barbecue plans. I know I always like to be invited places. It makes me feel good that people want to be with me. You can make your neighbor feel good and included, too.

August

National Friendship Day is the first Sunday in August. The holiday is an outstanding reminder to express gratitude for the friends you have. I absolutely treasure my friends because they replaced the family I lost. I thank them for every phone call, for every letter, for every visit to my apartment. Every one of my friends knows how much I care for them, because I tell them.

We risk losing friends when we take them for granted. As you'll read in my conversation with U.S. Surgeon General Dr. Vivek Murthy, he once became so consumed with work that he didn't make time for his most important relationships. "I felt ashamed to reach out to friends I had ignored," he wrote in *The New York Times*. National Friendship Day comes in handy because it's a gentle reminder to let your friends know how much you care about them.

Here's what I suggest you do on National Friendship Day: Write down a short list of friends. Send each one a text or an email. Better yet, pick up the phone. No matter how you reach out, the goal is the same: Tell your friends that you cherish them. Not only will they feel joy, but you will feel a surge of joy, too. (Expressions of gratitude have been proven to increase happiness.) A win-win proposition!

Gratitude has the power to deepen relationships and make them more meaningful. By telling your friends you're thankful for them, you're affirming their value. And who doesn't want to hear they're appreciated?

September

I received so much love from my grandparents during my childhood that when I became a grandmother, I was a superdoter! (One of my most treasured memories is the time I took my grandson Ari to an arcade and surprised him at one of those target-shooting games. Remember, I was a sniper. We came home with an armful of stuffed animals. He couldn't believe it!) The relationship between grandparents and grandchildren is so special to me that I've written several books about it and I'm now developing a concert, "Ruth Grandmother to the World," with my conductor friend Erik, the neighbor I told you about in "Friends and Lovers." And it's why I want to focus your attention on National Grandparents Day.

National Grandparents Day is held the first Sunday after Labor Day, and it's the perfect excuse for grandchildren and grandparents to spend time together. Since grandparents are usually the ones to give to their grandchildren, on this day, grandchildren can reverse roles and do fun or useful things for their grandparents—bake them a pie, watch a ball game together, help make their sluggish computer run faster. When grandchildren set aside time for their grandparents, their special bond has the chance to grow.

I'm very much aware, however, that not every grandparent gets to have these kinds of quality moments with their grandchildren. And this is why I also want to focus on the possibility of becoming a surrogate grandparent, if only for the day. Talk with your neighbor in advance. Offer to take her son or daughter for ice cream on National Grandparents Day. Ask the kinds of questions that grandparents often do—such as how they're doing in school and who their friends are.

There are formal ways to get involved, too. Many websites and Facebook groups are devoted to surrogate grandparenthood. Some even offer matching services. The New York City Department for the Aging, an agency I work with as New York State's Ambassador to Loneliness, has a Foster Grandparent Program that connects individuals who are fifty-five and older with children and young adults to support their academic, social, and emotional development. Not only does this reduce loneliness among older people by keeping them engaged in their communities, but it also helps reduce ageist stereotypes by fostering intergenerational connections. Similar programs are in place nearly everywhere—all you have to do is search for them to participate. When you do, not only will you feel good and have a good time, you'll be building a more connected community, and that helps everybody.

October

We didn't celebrate Halloween back in Germany when I was growing up. It's one of those holidays that hadn't yet made it across the ocean from America, though eventually it did, but long after I'd left. I've since enjoyed lots of Halloween parties. I once dressed up as Charlie Chaplin—complete with a suit, felt hat, and mustache. It was by far the best costume I've ever worn. I even imitated his waddling walk!

If you're feeling lonely, you might want to just turn off the lights on October 31 and pretend you're not home. But in the spirit of deepening your connections with neighbors, I urge you to think again.

Parents of young children tend to accompany their kids when they go trick-or-treating. This presents an ideal opportunity for you to show off what a fun-loving and welcoming neighbor you are!

Don some garish costume. When kids ring your

bell, greet them profusely as you give them candy. If you're dressed as a witch, give a loud cackle. Not only will the children appreciate it, but their parents will, too—and that's the whole point. The parents, not those little princesses and gremlins, are your real audience. My hope is that the next time you see each other, sometime after Halloween, it'll be that much easier to say hello.

November

I've always loved Thanksgiving because it's a major holiday but not a religious one. It binds all of us together and is inclusive of all religions, all denominations, even nonbelievers. But the pressure to come together may make you dread Thanksgiving. You may have nobody to share the day with, or maybe you feel anxious because you have to spend the afternoon and evening with family members who make you feel bad about yourself. I offer a few solutions.

First, adjust your expectations. Thanksgiving hardly ever looks like the idyllic gatherings you see in the movies. So much of the time families bicker, the turkey is dry, and somebody ends up in tears. Most dinners fall way short of what we think they should be like, and this is the reality check I want you to keep in mind.

Second, *be vulnerable,* but this time with your friends and neighbors. If you are not open and honest, not even with one friend, how will anyone realize that you have nowhere to go on Thanksgiving? Don't hide your situation. *Communicate your needs.*

And last, make a plan for next year. Very few problems fix themselves. You must be proactive.

December

The first day of winter is also the longest night of the year. This is why so many holidays in December are associated with light, to counterbalance all that darkness. If there's one lesson I've most wanted to pass along to you in this book, it's that you have the power to make your life bigger—and brighter.

If you are lonely, you likely feel the heavy weight of isolation. The world may feel very bleak sometimes. Listen to me: Do not give in to loneliness. When it is dreariest, when it is coldest and most gloomy, there will be warmth and sunlight again. Follow the advice I've given you, bit by bit. Just hold on for the thaw.

When I was in the orphanage in Switzerland, especially when the letters from my parents stopped coming, there were certainly days when I felt so unbearably lonely that I wanted to give up. My past had been wiped away and my future was very, very uncertain.

But look at me now. Nobody would have predicted— certainly not those who picked on me for being so ugly and short—that I would one day be a world-famous therapist or the first Ambassador to Loneliness of any state in America. Hold up my story as a light until you discover your own.

Life may be bitter for you now, but I am certain it has every chance of getting better. Change won't happen, though, if you hide in darkness. Work hard to cultivate the kinds of connections that bring happiness and meaning into your life. *It CAN be done.*

A Special Conversation with U.S. Surgeon General Dr. Vivek Murthy

DR. RUTH WESTHEIMER: I've shared a lot in this book about my own battles with loneliness. Readers might be surprised to learn you've also suffered from loneliness. At times in your life, you have lived alone, and you'd sometimes go days without seeing anyone in person. How did you start building meaningful connections?

DR. VIVEK MURTHY: I started building meaningful connections by being more intentional in my engagement with others. I was more proactive about reaching out to family and friends, even if it was for five minutes to say I was thinking about them. I also made the time we had together count by giving them my full attention; I wasn't always good at this, but I tried hard. And I made it a point to support or help a friend when they were in need. I realized that helping others was actually good for me—it got me out of my isolated cocoon and helped me feel like I had something valuable to offer the world.

RW: *The Joy of Connections* offers one hundred ideas and opportunities for creating fulfilling relationships. In your view, what is the very first step someone should take to feel less lonely?

VM: Cultivating connection doesn't have to be complicated—you can start by protecting a few minutes each day to reach out to someone you care about. You can express your gratitude to them, offer support, or ask for help. These small steps can make a big difference in how connected you feel and in your overall health and well-being.

RW: Too many people are embarrassed to admit they're feeling disconnected and alone. I'm trying to combat this kind of shame in my work as New York's Ambassador to Loneliness. What are you doing as U.S. surgeon general to address this big taboo?

VM: I've struggled with loneliness throughout my life and have experienced that shame myself. I issued a Surgeon General's Advisory on loneliness and isolation to have a more public conversation about an experience that millions of us have but are reluctant to talk about. I recently completed a college tour where I traveled across the country speaking to young people about the disconnection they're feeling and sharing steps we can take to build a more connected life. In speaking more openly about loneliness, we can help one another understand that we are not alone in feeling alone.

RW: Americans have been growing increasingly lonely over time. What moved you to proclaim loneliness an epidemic in the United States? The problem didn't start with Covid, did it?

VM: Although it was made worse by the Covid pandemic, loneliness and isolation have been widespread challenges for many years. I released a Surgeon General's Advisory because I was concerned about the severity and sheer number of Americans experiencing disconnection in their lives. I wanted people to know how common this was and how consequential it was to our physical and mental health. Being socially disconnected increases our risk of depression and anxiety as well as heart disease, dementia, and premature death.

RW: What's changed since you issued the advisory?

VM: Since it came out, cities, organizations, groups, and schools have been looking seriously at the loneliness crisis and working to improve connection and build community. Counties and states have put together strategies to address loneliness in their communities; members of Congress have worked to design policies to promote social connection; educational institutions are developing programs to help students build healthy relationships; and many faith organizations have shared with me that they are talking more openly about loneliness with their congregations. Loneliness is being recognized as a problem not only in the United States but throughout the globe. Last year, I became the cochair of the WHO Commission on Social Connection to start addressing loneliness on a global scale.

RW: My book is not about the physical health consequences of loneliness, but I realize they are considerable. Can you please outline what concerns you most?

VM: The health consequences of loneliness extend far beyond mental health to include physical health impact. Social disconnection is associated with an increase in mortality that is comparable to smoking daily and even greater than that which we see with obesity. People experiencing prolonged loneliness and social isolation are also at greater risk of diabetes and stroke, in addition to the concerns I previously mentioned.

RW: I've used behavioral therapy to help people overcome difficulties in their sex life. At what point would you advise someone who is very lonely to seek professional support?

VM: Loneliness is a natural feeling we all experience from time to time. It's like hunger or thirst—a signal that something essential to our survival is missing. But when loneliness extends for long periods of time, it can begin to impact our health and well-being. If your feelings of loneliness are persisting despite your best efforts, if they are making it hard for you to function in your day-to-day life, or if they are leading you to consider harming yourself in any way, that would be a sign that you should reach out for help to a trusted professional. You can always call or text 988, the mental health crisis line, at any time to get connected to support.

RW: You've admitted that after serving as surgeon general for the first time in the Obama administration that you felt particularly lonely. You wrote in *The New York Times:*

> I was suddenly disconnected from the colleagues with whom I had spent most of my waking hours. It might not have been so bad had I not made a critical mistake: I had largely neglected my friendships during my tenure, convincing myself that I had to focus on work and I couldn't do both.

So my question is this: Have you appointed your own ambassador to loneliness? (I discuss how important this is on pages 43–44.) Who looks out for you when you are working so hard?

VM: My wife is often the first to recognize when I'm really struggling. I also rely on my friends Sunny and Dave, whom I call regularly to talk about the issues that are most on my mind and heart. Years ago, we decided to form a *moai,* drawing on an Okinawan tradition where a small group of people come together to make an explicit commitment to have one another's backs. My *moai* with Sunny and Dave has literally changed my life.

RW: What gives you hope as we all work together to help people build more connected and meaningful lives?

VM: We all have a fundamental need for human connection. It's the common thread that binds us together. Everywhere I go, I find people are eager to talk about how to build more connection in their lives. I have encountered schools, workplaces, and mayors who are doing the hard work of building programs that will bring people together and nurture healthy relationships. I'm also encouraged by the fact that a little bit of connection goes a long way to helping address loneliness. The most powerful antidotes are often found right around us, in family members, neighbors, work colleagues, friends with whom we've lost touch but who are often just as eager to reconnect as we are.

Further Resources

I hope you have found *The Joy of Connections* helpful. To learn more about loneliness and ways to combat it, visit my co-author Allison Gilbert's website, allison gilbert.com, where she has curated multiple lists of additional resources, including books, articles, and organizations that are researching social isolation and helping individuals build more substantive and joyful connections.

Books

Loneliness has become a popular topic for discussion, and many books address this urgent public health crisis. I reference some of these in *The Joy of Connections,* while others helped me better understand the underpinnings of happiness and the formation of meaningful relationships.

In addition to the books I have mentioned, many others are worth exploring. A select group is noted below.

Brooks, Arthur C., and Oprah Winfrey. *Build the Life You Want: The Art and Science of Getting Happier*. New York: Portfolio, 2023.

Cacioppo, Stephanie. *Wired for Love: A Neuroscientist's Journey Through Romance, Loss, and the Essence of Human Connection*. New York: Flatiron Books, 2022.

Heng, Simone. *Let's Talk About Loneliness: The Search for Connection in a Lonely World*. Carlsbad, CA: Hay House, 2023.

Radtke, Kristen. *Seek You: A Journey Through American Loneliness*. New York: Pantheon, 2021.

Waldinger, Robert, and Marc Schulz. *The Good Life: Lessons from the World's Longest Scientific Study of Happiness*. New York: Simon & Schuster, 2023.

Studies and Reports

Social isolation is the subject of numerous scientific investigations. Researchers are analyzing the causes of disconnection and the profound ripple effects it has on our physical health and mental well-being. Similarly, they're examining the pillars of successful and fulfilling human bonds. I include a small number of these reports and studies here, some of which I have referenced in *The Joy of Connections*.

Boothby, Erica J., and Vanessa K. Bohns. "Why a Simple Act of Kindness Is Not as Simple as It Seems: Underestimating the Positive Impact of Our Compliments on Others." *Personality and Social Psychology Bulletin* 47, no. 5 (2021): 826–40.

Epley, Nicholas, and Juliana Schroeder. "Mistakenly Seeking Solitude." *Journal of Experimental Psychology: General* 143, no. 5 (2014): 1980–99.

Hall, Jeffrey A. "How Many Hours Does It Take to Make a Friend?" *Journal of Social and Personal Relationships* 36, no. 4 (2019): 1278–96.

Murthy, Vivek H. "Our Epidemic of Loneliness and Isolation: The U.S. Surgeon General's Advisory on the Healing Effects of Connection and Community." 2023. surgeongeneral.gov/connection.

TheLi.st in partnership with BSG and Berlin Cameron. "10 Minutes to Togetherness, 2024 Research Report and Tool Kit." Accessed May 12, 2024. 10minutestotogetherness.com.

Organizations

Stay informed and connected with leading experts and organizations dedicated to understanding and addressing loneliness.

Coalition to End Social Isolation and Loneliness
endsocialisolation.org

WHO Commission on Social Connection
who.int/groups/commission-on-social-connection

Foundation for Social Connection
social-connection.org

Global Initiative on Loneliness and Connection
gilc.global

Be in touch on social media

Dr. Ruth's X account is being updated by Pierre Lehu
X: @AskDrRuth

Allison
Instagram, Facebook, X, and LinkedIn: @agilbertwriter
YouTube: @allisongilbert

Monthly updates

Sign up for Allison's free monthly newsletter at allisongilbert.com/subscribe/. There, she will continue the conversation about loneliness and reveal even more strategies for developing and nurturing connections. She will also share updates on her other writing projects. I highly recommend it!

Email us!

We're excited to learn the strategies you're using to beat loneliness and live a happier and more meaningful life. Email Pierre and Allison at connections@allisongilbert.com.

A Timeline of
Dr. Ruth K. Westheimer's Life

1928	Karola Ruth Siegel born in Wiesenfeld, Germany
1939	At ten and a half years old, placed on Kindertransport train in Frankfurt to escape the Nazis, began living in orphanage in Heiden, Switzerland
1945	Immigrated to Palestine, changed name to Ruth
1948	Bomb blast caused serious injuries on twentieth birthday
1956	Arrived in New York on the ship *Liberté*
1957	Miriam (Bommer) Westheimer born
1959	Received master's degree in sociology from The New School
1961	Married Fred Westheimer
1963	Joel Westheimer born

1970–	Earned EdD from Columbia University
1979	Teachers College, studied to be a sex therapist, and opened a private practice
1980	Began radio career with taped show on WYNY-FM titled *Sexually Speaking,* which went live with listener calls the following year
1981–	Had radio show go national and became
1990	an icon, making frequent appearances on late-night television, writing books (*The Joy of Connections* is her forty-sixth), hosting several cable TV shows, appearing on the cover of *People* magazine, and giving lectures around the world
1997	Fred Westheimer died
2000–	Continued giving lectures and making
2022	appearances, taught at Yale and Princeton at the same time, published more books; play *Becoming Dr. Ruth* and documentary *Ask Dr. Ruth* produced about her life
2023	Appointed Ambassador to Loneliness by New York governor Kathy Hochul
2024	Published *The Joy of Connections* to address the loneliness epidemic

Acknowledgments

From Dr. Ruth

To the memory of my entire family who perished during the Holocaust. To the memory of my late husband, Fred, who encouraged me in all my endeavors. To my current family: my daughter, Miriam Westheimer, EdD; son-in-law, Joel Einleger, MBA; their children, Ari and Leora, JD, and her husband, Elan Kane; my son, Joel Westheimer, PhD; daughter-in-law, Barbara Leckie, PhD; and their children, Michal and Benjamin. I have the best grandchildren in the entire world!

Thanks to all my many family members and friends for adding so much to my life. I'd need an entire chapter to list them all, but some must be mentioned here: Pierre Lehu and I have now collaborated on two dozen books; he's the best minister of communications I could have asked for! And Allison Gilbert, an excellent reporter and writer, has been a true find as both a collaborator and a friend.

My neighbor who ever since my illness visits me twice a day, Maestro Erik Ochsner, and his partner, Masataka Suemitsu; my longtime friend, fellow board member, and "legal muscle" Jeff Tabak, Esq., and Marilyn Tabak; Cliff Rubin, my assistant (thanks!); my aides, starting with Shkurte Tonaj, who's been with me for more than fifteen years, as well as Tameka McLeod, Marcia Brown, and Arlene Wedderburn; Larry Angelo; Dr. Peter Banks; Peter Berger, MD; Simon and Stefany Bergson; Nate Berkus; David Best, MD; Tom Chapin; Frank Chervenak, MD; Richard Cohen, MD; Martin Englisher; Cynthia Fuchs Epstein, PhD; Nily Falic; Tovah Feldshuh; John Forster; my former neighbors and friends Raul Galoppe and Michael Berra; Meyer Glaser, PhD; David Goslin, PhD; Herman Hochberg; David Hryck, Esq.; Annette Insdorf and Mark Ethan; Steve Kaplan, PhD; Rabbi Barry Dov Katz and Shoshi Katz; Bonnie Kaye; Patti Kenner; President Jack Kliger and the other board members and staff at the Museum of Jewish Heritage, including Haley Coopersmith; Harold Kopliwicz, MD, and Linda Sirow; Robert Krasner, MD; Nathan Kravetz, PhD; Marga Kunreuther; Dean Stephen Lassonde; Matthew and Vivian Lazar; Rabbi and Mrs. William Lebeau; Rosemary Leckie; Hope Jensen Leichter, PhD; Judy Licht; Jeff and Nancy Jane Loewy;

John and Ginger Lollos; Sanford Lopater, PhD, and Susan Lopater; David Marwell; Marga Miller; Jeff Muti; Peter Niculescu; Walter and Debbie Nothmann; Dale Ordes; Frank Osborn; Rabbi James and Elana Ponet; Leslie Rahl; Bob and Yvette Rose; Debra Jo Rupp; Larry and Camille Ruvo; Rose Schreiber; Daniel Schwartz; Amir Shaviv; David Simon, MD; John Silberman, Esq.; Jerry Singerman; Mark St. Germain; Henry and Sherri Stein; Malcolm Thomson; and Maurice Tunick.

A special thanks to New York governor Kathy Hochul; New York state senator Liz Krueger; U.S. Surgeon General Dr. Vivek Murthy; our fabulous agent, Peter Steinberg, and his assistant Harry Sherer; and to all the people at Rodale Books and Penguin Random House who worked so hard to bring this book into the world: Matthew Benjamin, Mia Pulido, Kelly Doyle, Christina Foxley, Keilani Lum, and Cindy Murray.

From Allison

My greatest debt is, not unexpectedly, to Dr. Ruth Westheimer. We met for the first time when I was reporting for *The New York Times* on her becoming New York State's Ambassador to Loneliness. More than a year has passed since that initial meeting, and it's not hyperbole for me to say that she has become—after spending nearly every week since writing this book together—one of my most treasured relationships. I am honored that you entrusted me with this project and absolutely blessed to have been swept up into your expansive definition of family. You make everyone who knows you feel special, including me.

My gratitude also goes to Pierre Lehu, a wonderful collaborator. Your know-how helped coalesce the many critical threads presented here. The process of writing produced more than a groundbreaking book on overcoming loneliness and finding belonging—it created a new friendship, and for that, I am especially thankful. I am fortunate that Kate Buford and Tovah Feldshuh made the all-important introduction.

And while I will save you from repeating many of the names Dr. Ruth has already highlighted, I must double down on just a few. Profound appreciation to Joel Westheimer and Miriam Westheimer (and their families) for their outsize kindness and indefatigable assistance. And to Peter Steinberg, my literary agent at UTA: Your immediate belief in this book and bold advocacy for it were breathtaking. I am lucky to have your support and the backing of such a top-notch team. And to our editor, Matthew Benjamin: Thank you for championing this book with such urgency and care. Your counsel was wise and your thinking was clear. Every page was enhanced because of you.

To all the experts and authors who contributed immeasurably to this book, either directly or by providing resources and guidance, including U.S. Surgeon General Dr. Vivek Murthy, Judy Blume, Adam Grant, Dan Harris, Sunny Hostin, Gretchen Rubin, Wayne Baker, Cheryl Baker, Daniel Greenberg, Jeffrey Hall, Ryan Jenkins, Steven Van Cohen, Gregory Rose, Derek Penslar, Tom Worcester, Rob Maloney, Quill Kukla, Joseph Stramondo, Rabbi David Holtz, Ann Shoket, Sherry Turkle, Richard Weissbourd, and Julianne Holt-Lunstand. I also want to express my deepest gratitude to Traci Doromal, Katie Dealy, Jane Richter, and Rocio Cruz.

Special recognition to Abby Santamaria, Heather Clark, and Laurie Gwen Shapiro—dear friends who were sitting with me at a raucous dinner when the seed for this book began to take hold—and Lisa Belkin, Christina Baker Kline, Laura Mazer, Eve Kahn, Amy Reading, Carla Kaplan, Christine Cipriani, and Sara Catterall, who always lift me up and make me feel seen and valued. I am especially grateful to Bill Ferguson, editor exemplar at *The New York Times*. It's reasonable to assume that without our work together on "Dr. Ruth Saved People's Sex Lives. Now She Wants to Cure Loneliness," this book would not exist. I've been the beneficiary of your craftsmanship and expertise more than once, and for that, I count myself one very fortunate writer.

My dearest friends from elementary school, high school, college, and now—Kristin Brandt, Betsy Cadel, Tracy Costigan, Brooke Edgecombe, Nancy Friedman, Tanya Hunt, Holly Rosen Fink, Rachel Lehmann-

Haupt, Carley Knobloch, Deniz Ayaz Mullis, Jen Ross, and Janet Rossbach. You make my life bigger in all meaningful ways.

And to my family: Mark, my husband and best friend since we met at sleepaway camp, and Jake and Lexi, our smart, kind, and lovable children. You are worthy of the kinds of relationships that make you feel joyful and whole. The three of you are my most prized connections.

From Pierre

Thanks to my immediate family, who have supported me so much since the passing of my beloved wife, Joanne Seminara: my son, Peter Lehu, daughter-in-law, Melissa Sullivan, and my grandsons Jude and Rhys, and my daughter, Gabrielle Frawley, son-in-law, Jim Frawley, granddaughter, Isabelle, and grandson James Joseph; and to those friends and family who have helped me overcome my own feelings of loneliness, including the entire Seminara clan, Peter Zagare, and Gali Neufeld.

A special thanks to everyone who has made this book possible, starting with our agent, Peter Steinberg, whose own connections got us a deal within what seemed like seconds, and his assistant, Harry Sherer. Thanks to all the people at Rodale Books whose efforts helped us bring this book into the world: Matthew Benjamin, Mia Pulido, Kelly Doyle, Christina Foxley,

Keilani Lum, and Cindy Murray. And to my teammate with whom I spent so many hours laboring hand in hand, or should I say mouse in mouse, to formulate, write, and dot every *i* and cross every *t*, Allison Gilbert, thank you, thank you, thank you. Without your discipline, this book would be far less helpful to our readers.

And, of course, a great big thanks to Dr. Ruth Westheimer, whose minister of communications I've been since 1981. Whatever the status of your health, you're still finding ways to help people solve the problems that they face, even if it takes a Westheimer Maneuver or two.